100
Sermonettes

100 Sermonettes

Finding God in Everyday Objects

Rev. Henry B. Kleinert

100 Sermonettes: Finding God in Everyday Objects
Copyright © 2010 Rev. Henry B. Kleinert

Manufactured in the United States of America.

For information, please contact:

The P3 Press
16200 North Dallas Parkway, Suite 170
Dallas, Texas 75248

www.thep3press.com
(972) 248-9500
A New Era in Publishing™

ISBN-13: 978-1-933651-88-0
ISBN-10: 1-933651-88-1
LCCN: 2010912836

Author contact information:
sermonettes100@yahoo.com
www.100Sermonettes.com

This book is dedicated to my ten
wonderful great grandchildren in descending order of age:
Connie Kleinert, Tyler Kleinert, T.J. Kleinert,
Katie Cole, Connor Davis, Caitlyn Davis, Jackson Cole,
Samantha Ullrich, Colton Davis and William Ullrich.
Their ages are all the way from one to twenty!

Contents

Acknowledgments

I would like to thank my publisher, The P3 Press, a division of Brown Books Publishing Group, for helping to make this book a reality.

I would also like to acknowledge Dr. Charles Puls, who inspired me to go into the ministry.

Mostly, I'd like to acknowledge my wife of sixty-seven years and partner in the ministry for over fifty-five years. Both Helen and I loved ministering to children and loved to see the children's reactions to the objects mentioned in this book and what they learned about God's Word through my sermons

Last, I'd like to acknowledge the numerous congregations throughout the Midwest and North Texas. Thank you!

Introduction

I want to tell you a story about a time in my life where, for the very first time, I felt touched by the hand of God. It is a moment that is still so vivid in my mind. I was just twenty-four years old. A tornado had just ripped through the town, and there I was out on the Mississippi River. Who was I to think I could defeat nature like that? My canoe was almost straight up and down—frankly, it scared the heck out of me. The sky was dark—it crackled in that way that tears through your whole body. With nowhere to turn, I cried out, "Jesus, help me!" The wind stopped, and the rain stopped. We paddled toward this light, toward the shore. When we got to shore we found a little shack where they were helping people get across the river.

All of a sudden, I was calm.

In that moment, I realized there was something more. After all that had happened, everything turned out okay. There had to be a reason. The next morning I woke up, and the sun had come back, almost as fast as it'd left before the storm. I was very grateful to God in a way I had never been before; He saved my life after all.

That terrifying day out on the river changed my life. I began to recognize the power of prayer, something we all need to do. I still wasn't quite ready to devote my life to the cause though. It took a little extra convincing from a pastor I knew named Dr. Charles Puls.

I wasn't doing much with my life at the time—no aspirations to be an engineer or a firefighter or a lawyer or anything like that. It was really a time of searching. Dr. Puls must have recognized my uncertainty or just saw something special in me. Whatever it was, he put me on the spot, asking, "Have you ever thought about the ministry?"

"No," I told him.

There we were, just chatting, and he pointed his finger at me and asked, "Why not?"

Right there, I felt the Holy Spirit, even more strongly than I had on the river. It was right then and there that I knew I wanted to be a preacher.

It didn't happen right away, unfortunately—I had to go to war for a few years—but I got there as fast as I could. I finally started preaching in 1953, and I kept going until 2004. That was more than fifty years.

When I became a preacher, I found my way in life. It turned everything around for me. So you can see why it was always really important to me to give back to others by helping them find *their* way. I wanted to help all people—children and adults—so my message was one that speaks to all ages. With kids, you can start by getting them to Sunday school. After that you get them to sit through a service. I wanted to keep them interested so I'd do the children's sermons so that they could understand the word of God. It spread like wildfire! The kids would sit up, straining to see what I was holding up—whether it was a compass or a dollar bill—and they'd get excited about what I was talking about and that enthusiasm would spread to the parents. They wanted to know what all the fuss was about!

But the sermonettes aren't just for kids; they're meant to help you shift gears in a way. You'd be surprised over the years how many pastors would come up to me and say, "Remember that one about the bumblebees or the cross?" People don't always look back and say, "He made this point and this point about Advent or the Second Coming" but they remember how a blackboard relates to God's forgiveness. It helps them to learn and to absorb the message.

So I used everyday objects—things that would be memorable—because what you really want is to deliver a message that sticks with people. I would have hated it if one of my congregants went home and asked, "What did the Reverend talk about today?" I wrote about everyday objects because it opens your mind, and you start to make different connections. You're not thinking about theology. You're thinking, "How does this fit into my everyday life?"

I know well enough (after so many years of being in the seminary) what it's like to hear *a lot* of preaching. You've got to remember that the verses can be really confusing. If these items helped me, they can certainly help you.

One sermon that was the most meaningful to me was "The Cross." It tells us that God is up in Heaven, that He sent His Son here to Earth to die, and that we have a mission to make disciples of all nations. I really wanted folks to know that there was a Heaven, but that we have to remember that we're grounded here on Earth, and someday we're going to die. Right now we have to get out there and spread the Word.

At first glance this concept might seem simple. Jesus came to Earth. Jesus said, "Love your neighbor." Jesus died. But not all of the principles of Christianity are that simple. You really have to make these things relevant.

There's another important way to think about the everyday objects: God is not only present when you come to Him; He had a hand in everything. Without God, we wouldn't have caterpillars, birds, chalk, diamonds, corn seeds, pearls, trees, water, or any of the ingredients that make up all the things we take for granted. I wanted to show my congregants how to see

God everywhere and in everything. When you have the ability to see that, you truly have a life of abundance.

I've got letters from people telling me about sermons that have resonated with them. A lot of people loved the one about the three blind men touching the elephant. It's about how we all have a different view of Jesus and how He appears differently to all of us. The one about the caterpillar turning into the butterfly was also well-received. It touches on one of the most central aspects of Christianity: we have to die as our former selves before we become beautiful new creatures in Christ. Through all of this, I've learned that people tend to remember the things their preacher said when they were younger. That was the rewarding part—that I'm making such an impact on young people. I sure hope people will remember me many years from now.

Looking back, I feel really good about what I've done. I tried a lot of ways to reach people. Sometimes I succeeded; sometimes I didn't. One thing I've learned: there's a heck of a lot of good people out there that really care about me and about one another. I think one of the keys of my ministry is that I've been on the receiving end. I believe that these people are part of the call. As the senior pastor, my congregation went from around 800 people to 3,000 people. There could be any number of reasons for that growth but I have to think that those people were moved by my preaching. People have told me, "You were instrumental in getting Christ to be more real to me."

As a pastor, what more could I ask for than that?

Living a Christian Life

-1-

Are You in the Building or the Wrecking Crew?

Object:
Plate

Scripture:

Meanwhile his disciples urged Him, "Rabbi, eat something." But He said to them, "I have food to eat that you know nothing about." Then His disciples said to each other, "Could someone have brought Him food?" "My food," said Jesus, "is to do the will of Him who sent me and to finish His work. Do you not say, 'Four months more and then the harvest'? I tell you, open your eyes and look at the fields! They are ripe for harvest. Even now the reaper draws his wages, even now he harvests the crop for eternal life, so that the sower and the reaper may be glad together. Thus the saying 'One sows and another reaps' is true. I sent you to reap what you have not worked for. Others have done the hard work, and you have reaped the benefits of their labor."

—John 4:33–38

Think of the fancy china you save for special occasions. You may have fine porcelain or bone china, Spode or Waterford. Whatever the case, behind each of those plates is a great deal of planning and hard work: The right clay had to be found and brought to the factory. Then it was shaped, heated in a kiln, and painted. Finally, it was shipped to you. The results are long lasting, useful, and beautiful.

But what happens when an unruly grandchild at Christmas dinner smashes one of your beloved plates? All that hard work can be destroyed in an instant. Not only are you out a beautiful piece of art, but you also lose a useful piece of dinnerware.

We require the same deliberate, loving care to be shaped into good Christians. Friends, family, and members of the congregation can reinforce us, but one detractor with a hammer can shatter our spirit without giving it a second thought. A congregation—the teachers, altar guild, ushers, acolytes, choir members, library committee, stewardship council, youth workers—must all work together with one common goal: to do God's will. Using each other's talents and gifts, we can help each other and our neighborhoods with loving and caring projects "so that the world will believe," as Jesus said.

We have the opportunity to choose what we become: a person who builds up or a person who tears down. We, as Christians, are preparing for the kingdom of heaven by building a little kingdom of love here in this world. We do that by adding one little positive action at a time—one kindness, one act of love, one encouraging word.

So ask yourself: which crew am I in?

-2-

Trap of Temptation

Object:

A wine bottle, a loaf of bread, and a book

Scripture:

Then Jesus was led by the Spirit into the desert to be tempted by the devil. After fasting forty days and forty nights, He was hungry. The tempter came to Him and said, "If you are the Son of God, tell these stones to become bread." Jesus answered, "It is written: 'Man does not live on bread alone, but on every word that comes from the mouth of God.'" Then the devil took Him to the holy city and had Him stand on the highest point of the temple. "If you are the Son of God," he said, "throw yourself down. For it is written: 'He will command this angels concerning you, and they will lift you up in their hands, so that you will not strike your foot against a stone.'" Jesus answered him, "It is also written: 'Do not put the Lord your God to the test.'" Again, the devil took Him to a very high mountain and showed Him all the kingdoms of the world and their splendor. "All this I will give you," he said, "if you will bow down and worship me." Jesus said to him, "Away from me, Satan! For it is written: 'Worship the Lord your God, and serve Him only.'" Then the devil left Him, and the angels came and attended Him.

—Matthew 4:1–11

What are you going to be when you grow up? Do you want to get an education so that you can choose a good job? Maybe you want to be a lawyer, a police officer, or a teacher. Maybe you are just concerned about having enough to eat and just getting by. Or perhaps you're looking forward to having a lot of fun, drinking, and carousing.

Throughout our lives we are constantly making choices, from what to wear on the first day of school to what age we want to retire. It helps to turn to friends and family when we face tough choices: Should I move to a new city? Should I buy or rent? Should I try this drug that everyone else is doing?

In this kind of situation, it's important to turn to the right kind of people for influence. What do you say to the new friend who wants you to blow off studying for your midterm and go to a concert instead? What about making the decision to visit an ailing parent or go on vacation? Look to friends who have your best interests at heart: they will remind you that your education is important, that this may in fact be your last chance to see your mother. It's easier than you think to be steered wrong by someone with less than sincere motives.

There is nothing wrong with earning enough to eat, with having a fun night out with your friends, with a little pleasure. But Jesus tells us that there is more to our lives than just eating or having a good time. He said plainly that we are physical as well as spiritual. We are here not only to gratify ourselves, but also to make the world a better place.

Jesus resisted temptation by the devil. He was hungry, but He refused food. The devil challenged His godliness, but He refused to test God. The devil offered Him the world, but He didn't take the bait.

Would you pass the test?

-3-

The Empty Cross
(Easter sermon)

Object:
A real egg and a plastic egg

Scripture:
"You killed the author of life, but God raised Him from the dead."
—*Acts 3:15*

Every year starting in March, what do you see? Chocolate bunnies. Colorful baskets. Pop-up cards. Crosses in your neighbors' yards. Plastic eggs.

There is a reason that eggs have come to symbolize Easter. But let's think about two different kinds of eggs. There are the eggs you find up in the safety of a bird's nest or on a farm under the care of a mother hen. These eggs have life inside them; with the warmth and care of a mother, that life will be able to mature. But this process is delicate—too hot or too cold, and the life inside will die. Have you ever crossed a territorial mother bird around her nest?

Now think of the baskets full of eggs you collected every Easter as a child. They were hard and plastic on the outside—colorful, sure, and when you opened them up there was a nice surprise, but once you ate the candy (which you did immediately, no doubt) the fun was over. That egg produced nothing—no life was created.

After Jesus was crucified, He was placed in a man-made tomb. His followers feared the worst, but ultimately death could not hold Him. "I am the resurrection and the life!" He said. "If anyone believes in me, though he die, yet shall he live." Just as Jesus broke forth from the shell of death, we can choose to break free from a shell of apathy, indifference, and selfishness. Because we have life inside of us, we can be born again.

The church must be like an incubator. We must be warm, loving, and selfless so that we may develop those who have a long way to go to reach maturity. We must create the right atmosphere for people to break out of their shells into a new glory, born of hope and love. This is part of our purpose as Christians. Paul wrote to the Corinthians, "If anyone is in Christ, he is a new creation; the old has gone, the new has come!" Once we have broken free of our shells, we need to create a warm environment for others to thrive.

We're lucky. Without Jesus's sacrifice and the miracle of resurrection, we wouldn't have the chance to be reborn. But you have a choice. Do you want to be real, or do you want to be a shell?

There is nothing wrong with earning enough to eat, with having a fun night out with your friends, with a little pleasure. But Jesus tells us that there is more to our lives than just eating or having a good time. He said plainly that we are physical as well as spiritual. We are here not only to gratify ourselves, but also to make the world a better place.

Jesus resisted temptation by the devil. He was hungry, and He refused food. The devil challenged His godliness, and He refused to test God. The devil offered Him the world, and He didn't take the bait.

-4-

God's Word:
The Straight and Narrow

Object:
A piece of string with a weight hanging on one end (plumb line)

Scripture:

This is what He showed me. The Lord was standing by a wall that had been built true to plumb, with a plumb line in His hand. And the Lord asked me, "What do you see, Amos?" "A plumb line," I replied. Then the Lord said, "Look, I am setting a plumb line among my people Israel."
—Amos 7:7–8

In your lifetime, you've probably encountered more than your garden-variety pieces of string. String comes in all different thicknesses, lengths, and colors, and it's used for all different purposes. Think of everything you've ever used string for: tying your shoelaces, flying kites, playing yo-yo, making a friendship bracelet, putting a reminder on your finger.

Did you know it's also quite useful in the construction of a building? Construction crews call it a plumb line, but you might have used something similar working in the garage at home. Ever used a level to set a piece of wood straight before you drove a nail into it? A plumb serves the same purpose: it's used to check that the building is being built straight up and down. (Guess the architect at Pisa missed the memo.)

Imagine if a group of workers got a bit overconfident and decided they could work without a plumb line. If they were to step back and admire their work, they would probably insist it was straight. But if someone checked with a plumb line, they would notice the crookedness. Even if you destroy the plumb line, the building is still crooked.

You have your very own plumb line: the Bible. If you stick to it, it will help you to build your lives atop a solid foundation and continue down a straight path. God lays out the rules for you; you just have to follow them. Like a plumb line, God's Word will line up your lives in such a way that you will be as a beautiful temple. Think about it—to have a plumb line and *not* honor God would be foolish. When a workman sees that the brick wall is getting out of plumb, he changes the wall, not the plumb line. Unfortunately, it's difficult sometimes to accept our wrongdoings. It is usually much easier to blame the Word of God and just refuse to listen. Make the choice for yourself: what will you do when you get out of plumb?

-5-

Crossroads

Object:
A whiskey bottle and a cereal box

Scripture:

Enter by the narrow gate. For the gate is wide and the way is easy that leads to destruction, and those who enter by it are many. For the gate is narrow and the way is hard that leads to life, and those who find it are few.
—*Matthew 7:13–14*

Imagine you've got a bottle of aged whiskey in front of you. Right next to it, you've got a bowl of cereal. Both of these products came from the same source: grain. One—the food—sustains human life and makes us healthy. The other—the alcohol—makes pitiable slaves of millions. Same source, vastly different uses.

Human life is very much the same. We all begin the same way: we start as a tiny zygote, which turns into a fetus, and eventually into a tiny baby. As we grow up, some of us make healthy choices; we lead good and beautiful lives. Others make decisions that embitter and destroy others. Some people choose to bring others down with them. Every person has a choice.

One of the easiest choices you can make involves your perspective. There were two men who chanced to meet one afternoon. While strolling through a park, David Grayson, a Christian, sat next to a very unkempt man. Everything about him screamed *failure*; Grayson was determined to find out what brought him to this place. "I see you taking it easy in your garden," Grayson said. "My garden? Where did you get that idea?" the man struck back. "Are you not sitting there of your own free will?" "Why yes, there ain't nobody compelling me." "And can anyone by law make you move?" "No." "Well then," said Grayson, "I have proved, haven't I, that this is your garden—at least, as much yours as anyone's? Did you ever think that whatever you can enjoy can belong to you?"

"Say, neighbor," the unkempt man said to him, "I ain't particular, but are you all right?" Grayson paused, and then he asked him, "Have you ever seen the names carved in the wall by the city library? How do you feel about those names— Lincoln, Franklin, Newton?" "I don't feel anything," replied the man. Grayson told him, "I never go along there without wanting to take off my hat to them and say, 'Thank you, Ben Franklin, for flying that kite. It means a lot. Thank you, Edison, for inventing the light bulb.'" Grayson knew then what was missing for this man: he didn't have a sense of gratitude. He had a choice to make every day, and he decided that the world owed him everything. Grayson, on the other hand, knew that he owed the world a great deal more.

And he was all the better for it.

-6-

The Second Coming

Object:
Camera

Scripture:

Immediately after the distress of those days, the sun will be darkened, and the moon will not give its light; the stars will fall from the sky, and the heavenly bodies will be shaken. At that time the sign of the Son of Man will appear in the sky, and all the nations of the earth will mourn. They will see the Son of Man coming on the clouds of the sky, with power and great glory. And he will send his angels with a loud trumpet call, and they will gather his elect from the four winds, from one end of the heavens to the other.

—Matthew 24: 29–31

Think back to some of your old photo albums. (Do you even have photo albums? Maybe all of your memories are stored on a computer now.) Visualize that faded snapshot of you at four years old, sitting on Santa's lap. Turn the page: age seven, you and your older sister are selling lemonade on the street corner. Keep going: age eleven, you've just won first prize at the spelling bee. The winning word? C-o-n-s-c-i-e-n-t-i-o-u-s.

A little later: age eighteen, you're smiling from the driver's seat of your Jeep as you get ready to make the long drive to college.

The first cameras were large, boxy, and obtrusive, but they got the job done. The idea? To preserve forever a single moment. Cameras today still do that, only we have a great deal more options. Whether you have a disposable point-and-shoot or a fancy single lens reflex camera, the purpose is the same.

For the people in Christ's day, His birth was an important intrusion into society. Luke reported Mary's reaction to the miracle: "How can this be?" she exclaimed. After Christ was born, Herod even wanted to kill Him. None of them knew of God's long-term plan for Jesus.

The Second Coming will also be an important intrusion. This time, however, Christ will not come as a child, but as a judge. According to 2 Corinthians, "we must all appear before the judgment seat of Christ, that each one may receive what is due him for the things done while in the body, whether good or bad."

Take a moment to think about the big moments in your life: the birthdays, the baptisms, the graduations, the anniversaries, the good days, the bad days. Which of the big moments in your life do you think were the most memorable to other people? To Jesus? Are you willing to be judged yet?

-7-

Stay on Track

Object:
Compass

Scripture:

Jesus replied, "If anyone loves me, he will obey my teaching. My Father will love him, and we will come to him and make our home with him."

—*John 14:23*

Imagine you took a wrong turn somewhere, and now you're lost in the woods. It's dark—the middle of the night—you can see just the sliver of the moon above you, the wind is howling, and you can hear owls and insects calling all around you. You know that home isn't too far away, but you're completely disoriented. So you craft a survival tool from a leaf, a drop of water, and a paper clip. This compass is the one thing that will guide you back.

A compass points to a magnetic north. Regardless of which direction a person faces, the needle always points north. This simple tool (a high-tech one or the primitive one you make in the woods) has saved lives again and again when people have lost direction when the sun was hidden. To have a guide that stays constant is invaluable.

However, there are a few things that can knock a compass off its track. If it's near large quantities of metal, it can be thrown off. Large quantities of minerals can also render it inaccurate. And if it's between the magnetic pole and the North Pole, it will point 180 degrees off. For a tool meant to guide people to safety, that's a lot of qualifications!

In our lives God has given us direction as well. He has guided us, shown us the way, and prepared a place for us. He hopes that we will use our internal compass to follow His lead and find true salvation. However, like a compass, there are things that throw us off course. Worldly things can prove incredibly tempting; we want money, big houses, fast cars, sex, and exotic vacations. These are not wrong in and of themselves, but they can pull us off course and cause us to change direction—even get lost—if they become our focus.

Do you ever see bumper stickers or coffee mugs or t-shirts that say, "Live Dangerously!"? This has become a slogan for today's generation. Freidrich Nietzsche, a man who denied God and lived a morally mutilated life, said those now immortal words. He was promoting a life of adventure—kind of a slap in the face to those who value security, family, and spirituality. Nietzsche encouraged a life of abandon, suggesting we are captains of our destiny. He pushed aside the hand of God and suggested that everyone else do the same.

Clearly, Nietzsche didn't understand the danger of losing your soul. Consider for a moment which direction you are facing. Is it one that leads to God?

-8-

Always Looking Up

Object:
Compass

Scripture:

Therefore, since we have been justified through faith, we have peace with God through our Lord Jesus Christ, through whom we have gained access by faith into this grace in which we now stand. And we rejoice in the hope of the glory of God. Not only so, but we also rejoice in our sufferings, because we know that suffering produces perseverance; perseverance, character; and character, hope. And hope does not disappoint us, because God has poured out his love into our hearts by the Holy Spirit, whom he has given us.

—Romans 5:1–6

A compass has something inside of it that points to a magnetic north. Whether you're in Toronto, Rio, Sydney, or Moscow, it will always tell you which direction is north. From there, you can also determine east, west, and south. But what if you don't have a compass?

Many years ago, I was hunting in Colorado with an arctic training teacher. We were in a jeep miles and miles from our camp, because we had seen elk in the area, and we were

17

allowed to shoot what we needed to eat. When we caught sight of a small herd, I singled out a nice bull elk with the intention of getting him to come close to the jeep. I got closer and closer, but he must have caught my scent in the air, because he took off. I was too close to let him go, so I ran after him. I chased him as he bounded over a little hill, but eventually I gave up. It was late in the day, and I was farther from my jeep than I thought, so I turned to go back. But I couldn't find my friend. By that time it was dark, and I had no compass to guide me. So I looked up. I found the North Star, and that was enough to guide me east. Keeping my eye on the star the entire way, I found my way back through the dead falls, ignoring the snorting animals around me, and I found my way back to camp.

We are created in the image of God. Like a newborn that instinctively reaches for its mother, we can't help but look up. That night when I was lost in the woods, I was guided by a heavenly body. By looking up to Christ, we can always find our way home.

Jesus said, "I am the way." In looking to Him, we can be satisfied that we need little else. There is an old story of a king who had everything: a beautiful palace, a lovely queen, and many servants; still he was unhappy. When he asked a wise man what to do, the man said, "Go into the kingdom and find a perfectly happy man and wear his shirt for three days." The king searched and searched until he came upon a peasant whistling in the fields. "Are you perfectly happy?" "Why shouldn't I be?" the peasant replied. "I have a good wife, six healthy children, an comfortable cottage, and enough to eat. I am perfectly happy." The king asked for his shirt only to find he did not have one.

Both of these stories illustrate that by looking up, to Jesus, we can find peace. Happiness is not always catching the biggest elk or owning the most servants. When you get off track and lose sight of what really matters, do you know where to look?

-9-

What's Left on Your Rope?

Object:
A rope with a sliding knot

Scripture:

Sing, O Daughter of Zion; shout aloud, O Israel! Be glad and rejoice with all your heart, O Daughter of Jerusalem! On that day they will say to Jerusalem, "Do not fear, O Zion; do not let your hands hang limp. The Lord your God is with you, He is mighty to save. He will take great delight in you, He will quiet you with His love, He will rejoice over you with singing." "The sorrows for the appointed feasts I will remove from you; they are a burden and a reproach to you."

—Zephaniah 3:14–18

A man named Wally Lindgren used the following tactic to challenge his salesmen to utilize their time better. He showed them a rope that was 168 inches long; that was equal to a week with 168 hours. He wanted to prove to his men how little time they actually spent face-to-face with their customers: four hours. He slid the knot for each deduction; after deducting travel time, e-mail checking time, waiting room time, and coffee time (gotta have that venti skim latte with a shot), his men realized that they could double their earning power if they didn't waste so much time!

Now think about that 168 hours: how much of it do you spend worshipping God? One hour on Sunday. One hour in Sunday school or adult forum. Fifteen minutes per day in family devotions, equaling about ninety minutes per week. That's about 3.5 hours total. The Bible tells us we should love the Lord our God with all our heart and all our mind and all our strength. At 3.5 hours a week, are you meeting that requirement?

Now look at the rope again: 3.5 inches out of 168. That leaves 164.5 hours in your week! What are you doing with your time? It's easy to get caught up in the banal activities of life: paying the bills, shopping for groceries, retiling your bathroom floor, taking your kids to school and soccer and choir. You get so busy doing those things you have to do to get by, that you forget about doing the things you should be doing to really live. When was the last time you volunteered at a soup kitchen or nursing home? How long has it been since you browsed the prayer concerns list at your church? Do you go to Bible study? If you like to sing, have you considered joining your church choir? Do you pray with your children?

Take a look at your own rope. Are you giving God the attention He deserves?

-10-

Life or Death (Easter sermon)

Object:
A post and a tree

Scripture:

So, my brothers, you also died to the law through the body of Christ, that you might belong to another, to him who was raised from the dead, in order that we might bear fruit to God. For when we were controlled by the sinful nature, the sinful passions aroused by the law were at work in our bodies, so that we bore fruit for death. But now, by dying to what once bound us, we have been released from the law so that we serve in the new way of the Spirit, and not in the old way of the written code.

—Romans 7:4–6

When a tree is planted, it takes root, grows tall and green, and bears fruit. It sustains life for others as well (birds, squirrels, boys and girls coming for shade on a hot day). Now think of a post in the ground. It takes a lot of time and effort to paint it and prop it up, and once it splinters and rots, someone has to dispose of it.

We have the option of being like one or the other of these objects. We can be like the tree, continually growing spiritually and bearing fruit through evangelism and good works, or we can be like the post, spiritually dead and yielding no fruit but requiring a great deal of attention and care from other people. The difference between the two is a matter of life: the tree is alive, and the post is dead.

Easter is a time of contrasts: the theme of Good Friday is death, while the theme of Easter morning is life. We cannot revel in glorious Easter morning without remembering the tragedy of the preceding days. Jesus rose from the dead, so that we could live again. In celebrating that he died for our sins, we must remember that he died.

Jesus was crucified on Good Friday, a day of death and suffering. In remembering this day, we are reminded of corrupted justice, of the crooked actions of Pilate and Caiaphas. We are also sobered by the gory brutality, the scourging, the soldiers, the mob, the mockery, the deceit, and the hypocrisy of Judas's betrayal.

But there was glory to come; there was a light at the end of the dark tunnel, because Jesus returned. As much as we would like to forget it, there is no glory without the acknowledgement of sin and death. Paul wrote to the Philippians: "I want to know Christ and the power of his resurrection and the fellowship of sharing in his sufferings, becoming like him in his death, and so, somehow, to attain to the resurrection from the dead."

We too must experience separation from God. Christ said that anyone who loses his life will find it. So we must die to ourselves—choose to no longer be posts in the ground—so that we can live for God.

-11-

The Small Things

Object:

A radio and small TV

Scripture:

Now on his way to Jerusalem, Jesus traveled along the border between Samaria and Galilee. As he was going into a village, ten men who had leprosy met him. They stood at a distance and called out in a loud voice, "Jesus, Master, have pity on us!" When he saw them, he said, "Go, show yourselves to the priests." And as they went, they were cleansed. One of them, when he saw he was healed, came back, praising God in a loud voice. He threw himself at Jesus's feet and thanked him—and he was a Samaritan. Jesus asked, "Were not all ten cleansed? Where are the other nine? Was no one found to return and give praise to God except this foreigner?" Then he said to him, "Rise and go; your faith has made you well."

—Luke 17:11–19

It all started with the discovery of radio waves—electromagnetic waves that have the capacity to transmit music, speech, pictures, and other data invisibly through the air. Today a number of everyday inventions we take for granted utilize radio waves: microwaves, cordless phones, televisions, radios. Do you remember the early days of TV and radio? Do you remember the days *before* television? What about the Internet? Could you go a day without checking your e-mail or updating your Twitter page?

All of these "everyday" items were not always so commonplace. What started as Morse code—"What hath God wrought?"—took decades to evolve into the telephone. Radio was a wonder to Americans who listened, enthralled, to Roosevelt's fireside chats. Microwaves were a lifesaver to housewives who weren't gifted in the kitchen. And those tiny black-and-white TV sets were a big deal to the families who gathered around them in the fifties.

Those big things matter—they've made a huge difference in the lives of people all around the world. But now think about the small things. Emily Dickenson wrote, "It's such a little thing to weep, so short a thing to sigh; And yet by trades the size of these, we men and women die." She understood that it is the little things that make life more beautiful or sad. It's the little things that can truly destroy us. It's the little things that can break the spirit. Just one little straw, after all, broke the camel's back.

Our Gospel story is about gratuity. Ten lepers approached Jesus. Bonded by their misery and afraid to be seen in public, they begged Jesus to heal them, recognizing Him as the only cure. They had heard of Him—about the untold numbers of blind, crippled, and diseased people that He had healed. "Master, have mercy on us!" they cried. And He healed them. But only one returned to say thanks.

Saying "thank you" is one of those small things that often gets overlooked. This isn't just about politeness; it speaks of your character, that you have a grateful heart and recognize the little things that others do for you. What are the small things that matter to you?

-12-

Who Is My Neighbor?

Object:
Letters J, O, and Y

Scripture:

An expert in the law stood up to test Jesus. "Teacher," he asked, "what must I do to inherit eternal life?" "What is written in the Law?" He replied. "How do you read it?" He answered: " . . . 'Love your neighbor as yourself.'" "You have answered correctly," Jesus replied. "Do this and you will live." But he wanted to justify himself, so he asked Jesus, "And who is my neighbor?" In reply Jesus said: "A man was going down from Jerusalem to Jericho, when he fell into the hands of robbers. They stripped him of his clothes, beat him and went away, leaving him half dead. A priest happened to be going down the same road, and when he saw the man, he passed by on the other side. So too, a Levite, when he came to the place and saw him, passed by on the other side. But a Samaritan, as he traveled, came where the man was; and when he saw him, he took pity on him. He went to him and bandaged his wounds, pouring on oil and wine. Then he put the man on his own donkey, took him to an inn and took care of him. The next day he took out two silver coins and gave them to the innkeeper. 'Look after him,' he said, 'and when I return, I will reimburse you for any extra expense you may have.' "Which of these three do you think was a neighbor to the man who fell into the hands of robbers?" The expert in the law replied, "The one who had mercy on him." Jesus told him, "Go and do likewise."

—*Luke 10:24–37*

Take a look at these letters: *Y-O-J*. Mean anything to you? What about *O-J-Y*? Any better? Probably not. These words are meaningless when the letters are in this order. Look now: *J-O-Y*. It spells a very evocative word now, one that might just tug at your heartstrings or make you smile or think of someone you love. What if we make this an acronym, where *J* stands for Jesus, *O* stands for others, and *Y* stands for you. What I'm telling you is that if you put Jesus first, others second, and yourself last, then you'll truly find joy.

This text is one of the oldest and best-known parables. It's easy to understand. It is a story of contrasts, a lack of concern for human need, the love of a stranger, and how Jesus challenges us to reach out to people.

The lawyer asked Jesus, "What shall I do to inherit eternal life?" Doubt was not a concern; he did not ask if there was eternal life, he asked how to inherit it. The lawyer repeated the law: "'Love the Lord your God with all your heart and with all your soul and with all your strength and with all your mind'; and, 'Love your neighbor as yourself.'" It was one thing to know how to inherit life—the priest and Levite knew all of God's commands (*shema*)—but this parable demonstrates the importance of delivering.

The priest and the Levite put Jesus first, but they ignored their neighbor. Jesus taught that this was no way to inherit life. By loving your neighbor as yourself, you actually exude godliness. Whom are you putting first?

-13-

The Unity of Spirit

Object:

A balloon

Scripture:

Then we will no longer be infants, tossed back and forth by the waves, and blown here and there by every wind of teaching and by the cunning and craftiness of men in their deceitful scheming. Instead, speaking the truth in love, we will in all things grow up into him who is the Head, that is, Christ. From him the whole body, joined and held together by every supporting ligament, grows and builds itself up in love, as each part does its work.

—*Ephesians 4:14–16*

When you went to the dentist's office as a child, did they ever give you a balloon at the end for being a good sport (suffering through that filling)? Did you ever go to a birthday party and get a balloon giraffe from a clown? What about helium balloons with faces on them?—those get more and more clever every day!

A man was selling balloons on the street in New York back in the sixties. He would let one go now and then to get the attention of passersby and encourage business. He would let a white one go, then a red one, then a yellow one, and so on. A young black boy watched him do this for a while, and finally he came up the man, tugged his sleeve, and asked, "If you let a black balloon go, would it go up?" The man replied, "Son, it is not the color of the balloon that makes it rise, but what is inside."

God wants us to rise up. Just like the balloons, how high we rise does not depend on what we are on the outside, but what we are on the inside. Jesus said, "I tell you the truth, anyone who has faith in me will do what I have been doing. He will do even greater things than these, because I am going to the Father." Where did Jesus say there that His workers must have blonde hair, be at least five foot nine, have smooth skin, and be able to run a five-minute mile? Nowhere. His primary concern is that we accept Him into our heart and have faith.

This fourth chapter of Ephesians appeals to the mature Christian; it is about having direction in our lives and unity in the Spirit. It begins with a discussion of grace—God's gift to the unmerited sinner. Even though we have all sinned, He called us to be His own forever. What can we do in return? Use our gifts to spread God's message. We were all given special talents—preaching, singing, building, teaching, listening, painting, composing—and all of these can be used for worship. After accepting His grace and using our gifts for good, we must align our goals with those laid out for us in the Word.

God doesn't judge us if we don't wear makeup or have a full head of hair or straight teeth. What is important to God is that we live our lives in worship, as a reflection of the grace He bestowed upon us. Balloons come in some pretty fascinating shapes, sizes, and colors, but they are empty inside; it takes the outside air—or helium—to make them rise. Take a look at yourself: Are you living as a mature Christian? Are you floating in the direction of God? Are your goals aligned with His? Will you rise to the occasion?

-14-

A Time for Growth

Object:
An orange and a tape recorder

Scripture:

I am the vine; you are the branches. If a man remains in me and I in him, he will bear much fruit; apart from me you can do nothing. If anyone does not remain in me, he is like a branch that is thrown away and withers; such branches are picked up, thrown into the fire and burned. If you remain in me and my words remain in you, ask whatever you wish, and it will be given you. This is to my Father's glory, that you bear much fruit, showing yourselves to be my disciples.

—*John 15:5–8*

Have you ever tended to a garden? It's quite an investment. From a seed, an apple tree may take three to four years to mature and produce fruit. Raspberries planted in the spring can be harvested by summertime. But orange trees take full twenty-seven years to grow to maturity!

Now think about a tape recorder. If you speak into it— "testing, testing"—you can play it back immediately. You can record as much as you want, in small bursts or large bursts.

You can sing a song, recite a sonnet, or speak deadpan; the tape recorder stores it all in memory.

We are a little bit like both of these items. Like the orange, it takes us a little while to grow to maturity. We are baptized—usually as children—and the seed is planted. From that point on, we need to be reminded again and again about God. The message needs to be reinforced, so that it becomes permanently etched in our memory. We'll begin to feel confident saying, "Jesus loves me, this I know . . ." and we can eventually start bearing fruit when we tell others about God.

Chapter 15 of John is part of the last sermon that Jesus preached to the twelve disciples in the Upper Room. Our Savior gave instructions for all of his followers of every age, especially for us today. He delivered the message that if we are planning to go to Heaven, then we better learn the route. What's the route? The Bible.

Jesus's last sermon was very specific: the planting comes first, and then the growing. The message takes root when we first become Christians; even if we don't understand everything, the seed is planted. Jesus used the vine parable: He is the vine, and later on comes the branch. So we grow from the vine—from Christ. He is our life. To grow, we need to reinforce that original message that was planted. John wrote, speaking of Jesus, "If you remain in me and my words remain in you, ask whatever you wish, and it will be given you." So to grow we must read God's Word.

Are you still a seed in the ground? Are you ready to start growing?

-15-

The Plan

Object:

A camp light (with a red flasher on one side and a steady light on the other)

Scripture:

From that time on Jesus began to explain to his disciples that he must go to Jerusalem and suffer many things at the hands of the elders, chief priests and teachers of the law, and that he must be killed and on the third day be raised to life. Peter took him aside and began to rebuke him. "Never, Lord!" he said. "This shall never happen to you!" Jesus turned and said to Peter, "Get behind me, Satan! You are a stumbling block to me; you do not have in mind the things of God, but the things of men." Then Jesus said to his disciples, "If anyone would come after me, he must deny himself and take up his cross and follow me. For whoever wants to save his life will lose it, but whoever loses his life for me will find it. What good will it be for a man if he gains the whole world, yet forfeits his soul? Or what can a man give in exchange for his soul?"

—*Matthew 16:21–26*

What feeling do you get when you see a flashing red light? Excitement? Maybe if you're a child. Terror? No, not that extreme. A flashing red signals alarm or danger: Stop!—this a red light. Listen!—you have a message waiting. Stand back!—this explosive will detonate soon! A flashing red is not a light that guides, but rather it is a light that warns.

A steady white light, on the other hand, is like the Christian. Jesus said, "Let your light shine before men, that they may see . . ." What is that light shining within us? Jesus. This Light can open up a path in the darkness.

The Milwaukee Bucks had their own steady white light: a remarkable seven-foot-tall basketball player named Kareem Abdul Jabar. Today he is considered a legend. He was the pivot upon which the whole team rotated; four men watched as he did most of the point gathering.

Sometimes the Church is like that. The pastor is the star player, making all the important plays with little assistance. "That is what we hired you for, pastor" is a common statement.

At the end of His life, Christ had to flash a red light at His disciples. He had a plan; He had to let the world know what was about to happen to Him. So He began to show His disciples: He would have to go to Jerusalem and suffer by the elders and chief priests and scribes, He would have to be crucified, and finally He would rise on the third day. The plan of salvation involved the death of the Son of God, and Jesus knew it. Jesus knew why He had come to Earth: God wanted His creation to be with Him forever. And Jesus knew that in His dying, it was as if every sinner had died and paid for his sins. Paul wrote to the Corinthians, "For Christ's love compels us, because we are convinced that one died for all, and therefore all died."

Which light are you? Some people are flashy and attract a lot of attention—maybe they don't even mean to. As children of God, however, we want to reflect the steady light of Jesus from within us.

-16-

The Fulfillment

Object:
Four Bibles

Scripture:

I am the good shepherd. The good shepherd lays down his life for the sheep. The hired hand is not the shepherd who owns the sheep. So when he sees the wolf coming, he abandons the sheep and runs away. Then the wolf attacks the flock and scatters it. The man runs away because he is a hired hand and cares nothing for the sheep. I am the good shepherd; I know my sheep and my sheep know me—just as the Father knows me and I know the Father—and I lay down my life for the sheep.

—*John 10:11–14*

Four pastors got together a while back, and they discussed their preferred translations of the Bible.

"I like the King James version," one of them said. "It's traditional."

"I prefer the Revised Standard," said a second. "It's easy to read."

"The best is really the New English. This one is the easiest to understand," said the third.

The last pastor spoke up. "Those are all fine translations. I like my mother's though. She has translated it into my life."

We don't even know what version of the Bible the last pastor originally read; the reason it was so powerful for him was that it was brought to life. There are dozens of different English language translations of the Bible. So how do you know which one to choose? A classical interpretation? More modern and to the point? Today people are even translating the Bible with a political spin. Do you see the Bible as something that verges on boredom, or do you see it as a guide to abundant life?

God had no intention of leaving us to our own devices. We are His children, born of another dimension; Christ leads us. How does He do that? He leads us through prayer, worship, and the Holy Spirit. As our Shepherd, wherever He leads, we must follow. Eternity looms before us, but darkness becomes light.

Whichever version of the Bible you choose, what's important is that you lift the message from the page and apply it to your life. When Jesus says "go and make disciples," don't let that go in one ear and out the other. When He says, "love thy neighbor," step out of your comfort zone and help out a stranger. The words may be different, but the messages are the same. Where Christ goes, you should follow!

-17-

The Eyes of the Heart

Object:
A glass of water, half full

Scripture:

For this reason, ever since I heard about your faith in the Lord Jesus and your love for all the saints, I have not stopped giving thanks for you, remembering you in my prayers. I keep asking that the God of our Lord Jesus Christ, the glorious Father, may give you the Spirit of wisdom and revelation, so that you may know Him better. I pray also that the eyes of your heart may be enlightened in order that you may know the hope to which He has called you, the riches of His glorious inheritance in the saints, and His incomparably great power for us who believe.

— Ephesians 1:15–19

Think about escaping into your house on a sweltering hot day; all you want at that moment is something to quench your thirst. There's a glass of ice-cold water on the table, but someone has already drank half of it. Do you consider that glass half empty or half full? This is a timeless question, because it speaks to living your life with optimism and thankfulness. If you think of the glass as half empty, you're being negative; the water is running out. If it's half full to you, well, at least there's some in there!

This question applies to other aspects of our lives. Do we see the good in others, or do we see only the bad? Maybe you have a friend who has been there for you every time you call, every time you need help, but the instant this friend makes a mistake, do you throw her out with the bathwater? When someone cuts you off on the highway, do you scream, or do you remind yourself that maybe he's just having a hard day? When you fall on tough times, do you look for the light at the end of the tunnel?

Jesus took in ordinary people—fishermen, tax collectors, and tentmakers—and made them His disciples. This act of love, and of seeing the good in people, was how Christianity began. No matter what you do for a living, what matters is how you make a life. Do you have a heart for people who are sick, poor, starving, and distressed? Jesus did.

In the last couple of decades, the incidence of school shootings has skyrocketed. One boy took a shotgun and gasoline to school and said later, "I'm tired of living." He was hurting; all he needed was someone to care and be his friend. Someone to say, "You know, things may seem tough, but you do have some things to be thankful for. Let's see how we can make it better."

Let us not tease anyone for any reason. Let us do everything we can to bring some joy into the lives of boys, girls, and adults. Let us live in thanksgiving for the big things—our family, our friends, and our jobs—as well as the small things, like a sunny day or that nice woman you met at the coffee shop who, in two minutes of conversation, improved your whole day.

By injecting a little optimism and thankfulness into your own heart, you could be that memorable person who makes a huge difference for someone.

-18-

What is God?

Object:
A mirror

Scripture:

If I speak in the tongues of men and of angels, but have not love, I am only a resounding gong or a clanging cymbal. If I have the gift of prophecy and can fathom all mysteries and all knowledge, and if I have a faith that can move mountains, but have not love, I am nothing. If I give all I possess to the poor and surrender my body to the flames, but have not love, I gain nothing.

—1 Corinthians 1:1–3

Remember the evil queen from *Snow White and the Seven Dwarfs*? Every day she would look in the mirror and ask the same question: "Mirror, mirror, on the wall, who is the fairest one of all?" When the mirror said that Snow White was the fairest, well, things got ugly. The essential conflict of the story—the queen's jealousy toward Snow White—began because the mirror told the truth. Mirrors don't lie.

Think about what happens when you look into a mirror—you see a reflection of course. But that's only what's on the surface. You're not seeing what's inside, because the mirror knows nothing about what's in your heart. But God knows. 1 Samuel 16:7 says, "The Lord does not look at the things man looks at. Man looks at the outward appearance, but the Lord looks at the heart."

Dr. Menninger of the famous Menninger Clinic wrote a book called *Whatever Became of Sin?* In this book he suggests that, in healing from painful memories, tragedy, and our past transgressions, we have to face the fact that we have all sinned and fall short of the glory of God (Romans 3:23 tells us this). We must recognize our own sin before we can receive forgiveness. After all, what was the first thing that Jesus preached? "Repent, for the kingdom of God is at hand!"

Once we face ourselves as sinners, we can begin to understand who God is. So who is He? 1 Corinthians is very specific. This passage describes the importance of love: Speaking in the tongues of angels without love is just noise. Prophecy without love is just empty knowledge. Sacrifice without love is all for nothing. Later we are reminded that God's love never fails. Knowing what God is like, we should make it our goal to be a reflection of God.

God does not care if you're dressed to the nines or dressed in rags, if you're sporting a fancy new haircut or your head is shaved, if you're wearing a tailored suit or sweat suit, or whether your makeup is from SAKS or CVS. God can see straight through that double-breasted suit and pinstriped button up; He knows you spent a fortune on it just to impress your coworker. So take a moment to face yourself. Hold a mirror up to your heart and see it as God sees it. Are you satisfied with the refection?

-19-

The Flesh and the Spirit

Object:
Some jewelry, lotion, a curling iron, and perfume

Scripture:

. . . you have taken off your old self with its practices and have put on the new self, which is being renewed in knowledge in the image of its Creator.

—Colossians 3:9–10

Picture this scenario: It's six in the evening. The bathroom door has been locked for hours. A steady stream of laughter and the overwhelming stench of too much perfume and hairspray emanates from behind the door. One of the girls spends twenty minutes debating which of two identical earrings best matches her dress. After curling her long brown hair, another girl decides she'd rather wear it straight and has a minor meltdown. Two of the girls are worried their dresses are too similar. All the while, the men wait patiently downstairs, knowing there is no hurrying the eager girls.

Sound familiar? This is prom night. Once the girls are finished getting ready and make their grand entrance, it's still not time to go to the dance! First, it's picture time. There must be documented evidence of how good everyone looks.

Let's think back to that powder room. All of those items—the chandelier earrings, the lavender-scented lotion, the expensive curling iron, the makeup, the eyelash curlers—are meant to enhance and beautify. If my kind, warm, and loving friend from the nursing home were to get all dolled up like that, she would only become *more* beautiful (even though she doesn't need any of that stuff to be beautiful to me). However, do you think that if an unkind person were to use all of those items on herself, she would become more attractive? No! We all—women and men—like to be well-groomed, but a person must be beautiful on the outside *and* the inside.

We are born in sin: selfish, proud, unkind, and unloving. Our only concern is fulfilling our own desires. When we are born again of the Holy Spirit, we are new creatures: we have new hearts, new natures, new desires, and new love. New on the inside, we become more beautiful on the outside as well.

So how do we know if we have the God dimension? We know because there is a whole cluster of blessings that God bestows upon all Christians: love, joy, peace, patience, kindness, goodness, faithfulness, gentleness, and self-control. Others will quickly recognize these fruits of the Spirit emanating from our being; these traits make us truly beautiful.

Have you ever been told you look like your mother? Maybe your mother was beautiful, inside and out. But even if you're the spitting image, without the God dimension people will see right past even the most beautiful face.

-20-

Memories

Object:
A video camera

Scripture:

Yet to all who received Him, to those who believed in His name, He gave the right to become children of God—children born not of natural descent, nor of human decision or a husband's will, but born of God.

—*John 1:12–13*

Have you ever been to a family reunion where you all sat around and watched old home movies? Were you grateful that you had that camera around to record those precious moments—you learning how to ride your bike, that trip to the beach when your brother got stung by a jellyfish, your fifth birthday party where you smashed your first into the cake? (Maybe you weren't so happy to have some of those moments recorded!)

With the invention of the video camera, we can capture in time every occasion, from the most special to the most horribly mundane. The entire panorama of human experience is now a part of our recorded history. Great men and women, long since passed away, remain not only in our memory but also on film, ready for playback.

We all remember the big moments: the death of a grandparent, Dad getting a new job, a sister getting married, graduation, a serious injury. Memories are a part of our spiritual growth as well, because we remember, through the Word of God, who we are.

In 1929 Eddie Cantor lost everything in the great crash. He was sick in bed, despondent about his losses and his lifetime of scrimping and saving. He had lost all hope for the future. Finally, his wife reassured him, "But you are still Eddie Cantor!" That did it for him. He got out of bed, wrote a book of jokes, and rocketed to international movie stardom. All it took was his remembering who he was.

Jesus said, "The truth shall make you free!" Spiritually we grow, moment by moment, "born not of natural descent, nor of human decision or a husband's will, but born of God." We are never static spiritually; we progress and regress. We move upward or downward. We gain new cells of spiritual insight and slough off the old. The only way to do this, however, is to have spiritual food. That food is truth, and Christ is truth, which we glean by studying God's Word. Thus when the food of truth is our diet, we grow. Our eyes grow sharp to the needs of others, and spiritual muscles develop, aching to be used.

Remember that muscles grow stronger with use. You must constantly use your spiritual muscles—in prayer, worship, and service, for example—so that they don't disappear.

Every time you recall that mission you took to Mexico or that really inspirational sermon you heard, it strengthens you spiritually. Think about the memories you're making. When you hit the playback button at the end of your life, will you be embarrassed to watch?

-21-

The Small Stuff

Object:
A nail

Scripture:

But godliness with contentment is great gain. For we brought nothing into the world, and we can take nothing out of it. But if we have food and clothing, we will be content with that. People who want to get rich fall into temptation and a trap and into many foolish and harmful desires that plunge men into ruin and destruction. For the love of money is a root of all kinds of evil. Some people, eager for money, have wandered from the faith and pierced themselves with many griefs.

—1 Timothy 6:6–10

I heard a story once about a general who was leading his troops into battle. Both sides were evenly matched. Things were looking up. All of a sudden, the general's horse lost a shoe and started limping—there was a nail missing. So he pulled off to the side to help his suffering animal. While he was away trying to fix the problem, the battle shifted and his men lost . . . for want of one nail.

I have seen examples like this in my own life. A little boy

trips on the playground and scrapes up his knee, all because of an unruly shoelace. A car speeding down the highway instantly spins out of control when one tire blows out. A man sits on a chair and tumbles over, because one leg of the chair is unstable.

Sometimes these small things make a huge difference. Have you ever thought about how much it means to your mom when you say, "I love you"?

In 2001, *Reader's Digest* printed a very moving story called "Everyday Heroes" that speaks to how much the little things matter. In Clovis, New Mexico, Carolyn Kitchens watched in horror as her house burned down. A few days later, she was at work at the Kelly Bar and Grill, and she overheard some of the local men talking around a table. The men had heard about her recent tragedy, and one of them spoke up: "Let's build her a house!" That's all it took. The whole town—carpenters, plumbers, and electricians—donated their time and money to build her a house. No one was paid, though she brought the workers food from her restaurant. Why did they do it? "She is a special lady," they all agreed. One man's thoughtful suggestion turned into an act of kindness and sacrifice by the entire town.

God tells us that we should be accountable for every word we speak. Matthew 12:36 says, "But I tell you that men will have to give account on the day of judgment for every careless word they have spoken." That curse word that slipped out when someone cut you off on the highway the other day? That angry letter you wrote to the phone company when your service was less than stellar? That night you lashed out at your husband for coming home late? God hears all of this, even though you may want to forget it.

Jesus truly revolutionized thinking. He told us to turn the other cheek, love our enemies, give up our riches, be peacemakers, avoid judging others, and forgive again and again. Since we don't live in a vacuum, our actions affect others. Think about the words you say. Do they promote peace, or do they cause discord? Are you holding onto resentment, or do you forgive? You will be accountable for even the smallest action you take. Will you be able to explain yourself?

-22-

The Heart of Giving

Object:
A bagel

Scripture:

You were taught, with regard to your former way of life, to put off your old self, which is being corrupted by its deceitful desires; to be made new in the attitude of your minds; and to put on the new self, created to be like God in true righteousness and holiness. Therefore each of you must put off falsehood and speak truthfully to his neighbor, for we are all members of one body. . . . He who has been stealing must steal no longer, but must work, doing something useful with his own hands, that he may have something to share with those in need. Do not let any unwholesome talk come out of your mouths, but only what is helpful for building others up according to their needs, that it may benefit those who listen. And do not grieve the Holy Spirit of God, with whom you were sealed for the day of redemption. Get rid of all bitterness, rage and anger, brawling and slander, along with every form of malice. Be kind and compassionate to one another, forgiving each other, just as in Christ God forgave you.

—Ephesians 4:22–37

Think of the bagel you had for breakfast this morning (or maybe you had eggs or cereal). Did you finish it? If there was any left over, did you just throw it in the trash?

There's a lot we take for granted here in America. We have an abundance of wealth: fast cars, mansions, glamorous clothing, and food. We overindulge frequently, while there are millions of people all over the world who would happily pick up those scraps from your bagel.

As Americans, we have the ability to help. As Christians we have a responsibility to do so.

Jesus told us exactly how to meet God in this world before He comes again: "For I was hungry and you gave me something to eat, I was thirsty and you gave me something to drink, I was a stranger and you invited me in." God has given us so much, so we are to share with others who do not have what we have—even our enemies.

The sun gives us light so that we can live. The moon gives of its reflected light. The rain gives water to the plants of the earth. The air gives of its oxygen. The sea gives of its food. The trees give of their fruit and wood. The flowers give of their beauty and pollen. The animals, the birds, and the whole earth all have something to give. That includes us. As God has given to us, we are to give. When we do, He meets us in love.

The entire book of Ephesians is a solid book of direction on how to live a Christian life: what to do and what not to do. Paul wrote this book about 2,000 years ago, when the actions of humans were very much like they are today. It can be very difficult, however, to tune out all the distractions today that pull us away from God's instruction. For years mankind has been spiritually abused by art, drama, music, literature, philosophy, and most recently, psychology and religion. But Ephesians makes it clear for us. We are to speak truthfully. We are to stop stealing. We are to work earnestly. We are to live compassionately. Compassionate living includes giving to the less fortunate.

When we live in a society that so highly values wealth and consumption, it's not always easy to give of yourself. Start by tuning out the messages that attempt to discourage you. Make a small donation to your favorite charity. You're already one step closer to God.

-23-

God's Call

Object:
A ticking clock

Scripture:

Be very careful, then, how you live—not as unwise but as wise, making the most of every opportunity, because the days are evil.

—*Ephesians 5:15–16*

Every day comes and every day goes. The sun comes up even if you're still asleep. The sun sets even if it's behind the clouds. There are the same amount of hours in every day; a clock just helps us organize them all. Where should we go? What should we be doing?

The most precious gift that we have to give is our time. Why? Because we have a limited amount, and we can never get it back. Once you waste an hour watching trash TV or reading gossip magazines, you can never get that hour back.

This is why it's important to go out of our way to spend our time (and money) wisely. Perhaps you would feel a little guilty about spending half your paycheck on a new flat screen TV. But what if you spent that same money on food, gas, and a hotel to visit a loved one? Take time every day to pray for the people you care about. Take a few moments to tell your mothers and fathers, brothers and sisters, husbands and wives, that you love them. It takes about three seconds to say, "I love you, Grandma." It might not mean much to you, but it will make her day.

So what happens when you get distracted and you don't spend your time wisely?

A horse trader in Nebraska had a reputation for training horses and mules. Nearby, a farmer was dealing with an incorrigible mule that defied training; he turned to the trader for help. The trainer told him, "Treat him with love and kindness." So the farmer tried a new method: he curried him down and gave him special oats. This didn't work. Losing hope, he begged the trainer to come to his farm in person. The trainer arrived, picked up a two-by-four, and smacked the disobedient mule right between the eyes.

"Wait a minute! You said to treat him with love and kindness!" cried the farmer.

"Right. But first you have to get his attention."

When God needs to get our attention, sometimes He has to be a little more direct. Perhaps it's an illness, a tragedy, or the loss of a job. Radio and TV minister Joni Eareckson experienced God's wake-up call firsthand: she was paralyzed in a diving accident as a teenager. Luckily, she saw it for what it was: a call to be more grateful and use her precious time for good. "I thank God that I am what I am," she said, "for God has used me in so many wonderful ways to reach many people in Christ."

Hopefully, God will never have to go to such dramatic lengths to get your attention. Hopefully, you're already living each of your days to the fullest, loving one another and living in fellowship. It has been said that we can't do anything about tomorrow, for it is not yet here. Nor can we do anything about yesterday, for it is past. Are you making the most of right now?

-24-

Layer by Layer

Object:
A ceramic cup

Scripture:

When the time of their purification according to the Law of Moses had been completed, Joseph and Mary took Him to Jerusalem to present Him to the Lord (as it is written in the Law of the Lord, "Every firstborn male is to be consecrated to the Lord") . . . When Joseph and Mary had done everything required by the Law of the Lord, they returned to Galilee to their own town of Nazareth. And the child grew and became strong; He was filled with wisdom, and the grace of God was upon Him.

—Luke 22:22– 24, 39, 40

Have you ever been to a tea party, or maybe just a really fancy restaurant that served coffee and tea and nice china? Do you know what went into creating that beautiful teacup? Someone molded it from clay and then painstakingly painted that intricate design on it. Then it was put into a kiln and fired again and again and again, where the colors became permanent. Each time the cup was fired, it became stronger.

Then it came to you. No matter how hard you scrub it clean, that pretty design won't wash off.

We are like that ceramic cup: As the years go by, we are gradually hardened into what we become for the rest of our lives. We face trials and tribulations, ups and downs, but each time we turn to God for guidance, we are built up stronger. The end result is multi-layered person who has been through the fire and came out stronger.

I want to share a poem with you, one written by a teacher in Madison, Wisconsin:

> *I took a piece of plastic clay and idly fashioned it one day*
> *And, as my fingers pressed it, still it moved and yielded to will*
> *I came again when days were past;*
> *the bit of clay was hard at last*
> *The form I gave it still it bore, but I could that form no more*
> *I took a piece of living clay and deftly formed it day by day*
> *And molded, with my power and*
> *art a young child's soft and yielding heart*
> *I came again when years were gone; it was a man I looked upon*
> *He still that early impress bore, but I could change it nevermore*

See? We are just like that ceramic cup. There are more and more studies of what happens in infancy—that children absorb so much at that age that it molds them permanently into what they will be for a lifetime. Proverbs 22:6 says, "Train a child in the way he should go, and when he is old he will not turn from it." That's very important, because it means that we have a duty to instill our children with good values right away. Of course they will get older and add layers of hardness, but that original shape cannot be changed.

Think now about what happens to a china cup if you accidentally tap it against a sharp ledge. It chips! Humans can chip too, when we fall away from God for a period of time. When we go to church, worship, and read the Bible, however, we continually build up those layers so that it's harder for us to crack. Will you be prepared when someone tries to chip away at you, or worse—shatter you completely?

-25-

The Big Picture

Object:
Binoculars

Scripture:

In the sixth month, God sent the angel Gabriel to Nazareth . . . to a virgin pledged to be married to a man named Joseph. The angel went to her and said, "Greetings, you who are highly favored! The Lord is with you." Mary was greatly troubled at his words . . . But the angel said to her, "Do not be afraid, Mary, you have found favor with God. You will be with child and give birth to a son, and you are to give Him the name Jesus. He will be great and will be called the Son of the Most High. The Lord God will give Him the throne of his father David, and He will reign over the house of Jacob forever; His kingdom will never end." "How will this be," Mary asked the angel, "since I am a virgin?" The angel answered, "The Holy Spirit will come upon you, and the power of the Most High will overshadow you. So the holy one to be born will be called the Son of God. . . . For nothing is impossible with God." "I am the Lord's servant," Mary answered. "May it be to me as you have said."
—Luke 1:26–38

Have you ever sat in the nosebleed section at a baseball game, where you were so high up that the players looked like ants? Swing and a miss? Wait, no! I think he's running!

Today, most stadiums have huge screens that you can watch to see what's happening. (The screen at the new Cowboy Stadium is even bigger than the field!) Back in the day, however, you could improve your situation by using binoculars. You peek through the tiny eyeholes, and the object on the other side is magnified. But what happens if you look through binoculars backward? The object appears much smaller.

The Bible works very much like this. We need to read and study the Bible with an open heart that seeks to understand the words on the page. When we come with that mindset, the message will become clear and we will be drawn deeper and deeper in. On the other hand, if you look to the Bible the wrong way—trying to find excuses for your wrongdoings— then it will just feel like work, and you will find the wrong answers. Not even the most thorough probing through the pages of the Bible will tell you that it's OK to steal from your brother. No amount of days spent reading in seclusion will justify you having an affair. And nowhere in the Bible—New or Old Testament—will excuse you from your Christian duties of going to church, worshipping God, and praying.

Do you remember how Mary reacted when the angel told her she was going to give birth to Jesus? She was skeptical, of course. As a virgin, she thought it was impossible! But she opened her heart to the message she was hearing. She didn't stare at the angel, stone-faced, and refuse to listen. She accepted her responsibility and told him, "My soul magnifies the Lord."

A man once walked in on Mark Twain reading the Bible; as Twain was a noted atheist, the man was taken aback and asked what he was doing. "I'm trying to find the loopholes," Twain told him.

When you read the Bible, what are you looking for?

-26-

Turn Up the Heat

Object:
A thermostat

Scripture:
Don't just pretend to love others. Really love them. Hate what is wrong. Hold tightly to what is good. Love each other with genuine affection, and take delight in honoring each other. Never be lazy, but work hard and serve the Lord enthusiastically. Rejoice in our confident hope. Be patient in trouble, and keep on praying. When God's people are in need, be ready to help them. Always be eager to practice hospitality.
—Romans 12:9–13

Remember when you got sick as a child and your mother patted your forehead to see if you had a fever? That method is tried-and-true, but a bit rudimentary. A more accurate way to check the temperature is to use a thermometer. You can stick it in a person's ear or mouth to check for fever, you can attach it to the front of your house to check the weather, or you can spear it into a juicy roast to check if it's reached the perfect temperature. One thing about a thermometer, however, is that it's a pretty limited instrument: it can't make it more hot or cold, it merely *tells* you what the temperature is.

Now consider a thermostat. Have you ever ridden in a car with a group of people, each of whom had a different comfort level when it came to the temperature? "Can you turn the heat up a little, please?" "No, no, more A/C!" A thermostat doesn't just read the environment, it *controls* it. It's hooked up to the furnace or air conditioner, so it has the ability to regulate heat and cold.

Which of these instruments are you more like?

Years ago, a man blew up the physics lab at the University of Wisconsin. The blast was far-reaching, shattering the stained-glass windows at Luther Memorial a half-mile away. People were devastated. Many of them drove by, saw the damage, grieved to themselves, and kept on driving. They reported the bad news to others, like a thermometer saying the environment is cold, cold, cold! But a few people stepped up. They offered their time and money and found an artist to fix the windows, finally repairing the damage. They didn't just watch and wait for someone else to turn the heat up.

It's easy to talk about what's going wrong in the world: We're fighting multiple wars. Our economy is failing. Our education system is struggling. Our neighborhoods are mired in poverty. The Church is being forced to defend itself. Are you going to do anything about it? Are you going to just sit back and watch, throwing out opinions but offering no real solutions?

Like thermostats, we have the ability to change our environment. You may feel helpless in the face of some of the great problems of the world, but you can start small in your own neighborhood. Start by being a little bit more loving, kind, and caring. Tell people about Jesus. We can change our homes, our schools, and our churches by setting a climate of love.

-27-

The Morning Star

Object:

A cup

Scripture:

For this very reason, make every effort to add to your faith goodness; and to goodness, knowledge; and to knowledge, self-control; and to self-control, perseverance; and to perseverance, godliness; and to godliness, brotherly kindness; and to brotherly kindness, love. For if you possess these qualities in increasing measure, they will keep you from being ineffective and unproductive in your knowledge of our Lord Jesus Christ. But if anyone does not have them, he is nearsighted and blind, and has forgotten that he has been cleansed from his past sins. Therefore, my brothers, be all the more eager to make your calling and election sure. For if you do these things, you will never fall, and you will receive a rich welcome into the eternal kingdom of our Lord and Savior Jesus Christ.

—2 Peter 1:5–11

Why do we use cups? To drink, of course. A plate can't contain liquid. The oceans, lakes, and rivers are all contained by shorelines, because liquid can't contain itself. What would you do without your favorite mug to contain your hot coffee in the morning?

A cup needs a handle so that it can be held. It also needs a power outside of itself to get the liquid into the cup. That iced tea doesn't magically appear in that glass to quench your thirst!

We are like a cup: We have been filled with the water of life—we contain it—and therefore we can help someone who is thirsty. There is an overwhelming amount of suffering in this world, but we have within our hearts the living water. Just a little bit can really provide a lot for the world. Think of all the missionaries who put their lives on hold to go out to the most impoverished places on the earth. For someone who has been without food and water, who has never heard the good news of God, and who has never had a kind soul give him the time of day, this can mean the world.

Jesus said, "I can make you a river of living water." God wants us to overflow with love for others. He doesn't want us to offer a drop. He doesn't want us to offer a thimbleful. Not even a small cup. He wants us to overflow like a river that recently flooded. We are to give freely of the love in our hearts. We should share our time, our talents, and our money.

Our scripture speaks to cultivating the fruits of the Spirit. God doesn't want you to be merely good. He wants you to be good and faithful. He doesn't want you to then gain self-control but forgo perseverance. And He would hate for you to skip out on godliness. To be productive and effective in learning about Christ, the scripture says, you must overflow with all of these qualities. Otherwise, you are "nearsighted and blind."

Jesus said, "And if anyone gives even a cup of cold water to one of these little ones because he is my disciple, I tell you the truth, he will certainly not lose his reward." Now, he is not saying you have to actually stand on the street corner and hand out cups of water to people who are thirsty. Sharing love is just as important. Take some to reflect on your own cup: Is it overflowing? If it is, what are you passing on?

-28-

More than but a Shell

Object:
A doll

Scripture:

Be stunned and amazed, blind yourselves and be sightless; be drunk, but not from wine, stagger, but not from beer. The Lord has brought over you a deep sleep: He has sealed your eyes (the prophets); He has covered your heads (the seers). For you this whole vision is nothing but words sealed in a scroll. . . . The Lord says: "These people come near to me with their mouth and honor me with their lips, but their hearts are far from me. Their worship of me is made up only of rules taught by men.

—*Isaiah 29:9–13*

Did you ever play with dolls as a child? (If you're a man, I'm sure you've at least seen them.) Dolls have eyes, hair, hands, and toes. These days, they are strangely lifelike: you can get dolls that cry, that eat, that urinate, that sleep, that spit up— nearly everything real babies do! You can dress them in any manner of clothing: a princess, a tennis player, a bride, a rock star, a flight attendant, a nurse. You can put makeup on them and dye their hair. You can decorate a home for them and find them a husband. In so many ways, they are like a little mini-person. But they are not real. They have everything . . . but life.

Dolls can do no wrong, but they can do no right either. They have eyes that can't see, ears that can't hear, and hands that can't heal.

Jesus said, "I have come that they may have life, and have it to the full." He didn't want us to be shells of people that look great but are helpless. God gave us the very freedom to choose how we live our lives; that freedom has a lot of implications for how we live our lives. When we make choices that lift us closer to God, it brings with it a great deal of joy, but we inevitably make decisions that bring grief as well. We can choose to go to church, or we can choose to stay home on Sunday morning. We can be selfish, or we can be selfless. We can attempt marital counseling, or we can settle for divorce as an easy out. We can conform to the ills around us—smoking and drinking—or we can honor our bodies. These are the realities of life.

Our scripture tells us how we should honor God. He wants us to be so in awe that we are blind, drunk, and staggering. He condemns the man who praises him with his lips and mouth but not with his heart. That person is but a shell—a doll.

Have you ever seen the Russian matryoshka dolls? You open up one layer, and inside there is another doll? Inside that one there is yet a smaller doll, and another, and another, and another? When you finally get to inside, what do you find? Nothing. That is not God's plan for us. Christ gave us heart and a new birth, so that we would be vibrant, overflowing with love, and able to bear fruit. What are you made of?

-29-

The Branch That Bears Fruit

Object:
A nametag

Scripture:

As the Father has loved me, so have I loved you. Now remain in my love. If you obey my commands, you will remain in my love, just as I have obeyed my Father's commands and remain in his love. I have told you this so that my joy may be in you and that your joy may be complete. . . . You are my friends if you do what I command. I no longer call you servants, because a servant does not know his master's business. Instead, I have called you friends, for everything that I learned from my Father I have made known to you. You did not choose me, but I chose you and appointed you to go and bear fruit—fruit that will last.

—John 15:9–16

Have you ever gone to a conference where everybody had to wear a nametag? Maybe you had to do that on the first day of school when you were young. Teachers and leaders do this so that people have a way of knowing who everyone is.

But you are more than your name. If someone says to you, "Tell me about yourself," what do you say? Maybe you talk about where you grew up. Your secret dream of becoming a Hollywood movie star. The fact that you're the youngest of seven siblings. Your irrational fear of butterflies.

Would you talk about being a Christian? That's an important aspect of who you are!

The Bible tells us exactly who we are. Genesis says, "Let us make man in our image." Created in the likeness of God, it would seem we can't help but know Him; there has never been a race or tribe discovered that did not have some idea of God. Adam knew God, yet he chose to rebel. Romans 3:23 reflects this problem about man: "All have sinned and fall short of the glory of God."

Because of free will, we can choose to sin or not to sin. Galatians 6:7–8 warns, "Do not be deceived: God cannot be mocked. A man reaps what he sows. The one who sows to please his sinful nature, from that nature will reap destruction; the one who sows to please the Spirit, from the Spirit will reap eternal life."

So what will you do with so many choices? You can sow anger and hopelessness and spread that around the world. Or you can sow the fruits of the Spirit—love, joy, peace, patience, kindness, goodness, faithfulness, gentleness, and self-control. We are told our task is to connect as many people as possible to God. We are to bear fruit—to make as many Christians as possible. Don't you want to be the branch that bears fruit for the kingdom?

Everyone who receives Jesus as Lord is a child of God. Because we are His children, God has a plan for each of us; He wants only the very best. Next time you're asked to wear a nametag, think about what you'll write. You are a child of God. Would you write that on your nametag?

-30-

The Coming of the Lord

Object:
A hammer

Scripture:

In the last days, the mountain of the Lord's temple will be established as chief among the mountains; it will be raised above the hills, and all nations will stream to it. . . . He will judge between the nations and will settle disputes for many peoples. They will beat their swords into plowshares and their spears into pruning hooks. Nation will not take up sword against nation, nor will they train for war anymore. Come, O house of Jacob, let us walk in the light of the Lord.
—Isaiah 2:1–5

A hammer is a pretty important tool. Imagine trying to build a chair, or a table, or a house without a hammer. It can pound nails into wood, thus holding boards together. It can also tear pieces of wood apart by pulling out the nails. It can be used to build up or tear down.

People are like this hammer: we can build others up or tear them down. God's hope for us is that we build, care, share, and love. God has designed us and He will use anyone who asks. ("I chose you and appointed you to bear fruit.") As we prepare for the coming of Jesus, God wants all of us—young and old, men and women, boys and girls—to perform acts of love, building up His kingdom.

For 2,000 years, men and women of God have been predicting that the Lord will come soon. It is the dream of those of us who love God that we will see the day when wars are no more and all men are living together in peace. But we are not there yet.

The world today is in turmoil. Over the last century, nations have fought each other continually: the Spanish-American War, World Wars I and II, Korea, Vietnam, the Gulf Wars, and now Iraq and Afghanistan. The Middle East has been embroiled in daily violence for decades. Thousands of innocent people have died of starvation and violence in Darfur. Tyrants have come to power in a number of nations, terrorizing their helpless citizens. The threat of terrorism looms over the air, rail, and underground commutes of millions worldwide. And nuclear weapons are dangerously close to slipping into the wrong hands.

Is this what God had in mind when He sent us to build up His kingdom?

Matthew 15:19 says, "For out of the heart come evil thoughts, murder, adultery, sexual immorality, theft, false testimony, slander." What does that mean? The heart of man must change. We must orient ourselves toward the heart of God. Jesus said, "Unless one is born again, he cannot see the kingdom of God." That's quite a strong message. We should be here on Earth, preparing feverishly for the coming of the Lord. God knows what is truly in our hearts.

Many years ago a teacher in DeLaSalle high school asked his students to write their obituaries. He told the students not to be concerned with how long their column was; what mattered was whether the world thought they were important. Will anyone remember a story about kindness or forgiveness?

-31-

That's the Spirit!

Object:
Incense

Scripture:

And so John came, baptizing . . . and preaching a baptism of repentance for the forgiveness of sins. . . . All the people of Jerusalem went out to him. Confessing their sins, they were baptized by him in the Jordan River. . . . And this was his message: "After me will come one more powerful than I, the thongs of whose sandals I am not worthy to stoop down and untie. I baptize you with water, but He will baptize you with the Holy Spirit." At that time Jesus came from Nazareth in Galilee and was baptized by John in the Jordan. As Jesus was coming up out of the water, He saw heaven being torn open and the Spirit descending on Him like a dove. And a voice came from Heaven: "You are my Son, whom I love; with you I am well pleased."

— Mark 1:4–11

Have you ever been in a room lit with incense? You walk in the door, and you immediately know there is something wonderful burning, but you don't always know what it is. You can't see it or touch it, but you know it's there.

The Bible tells us that our prayers are like incense: "May my prayer be set before you like incense."

God's Holy Spirit is like incense. You cannot see it or even feel it, but it is very much there. Prayer can be incredibly powerful. I have always had prayer partners, some of whom live miles and miles away. The distance doesn't matter. I remember one of them had a daughter who was rebellious—typical teenage stuff—but her parents were very worried about her, so they asked us to pray for her. She is now considering the mission field. Another friend was having problems in her marriage. They had tried and tried on their own to resolve their problems; finally she turned to prayer and asked us for help. They are now very happy again.

Love, along with the other fruits of the Spirit, is the same way. You can't see it. You can't hear it. You can't reach out and touch love. But you know when love is in the air. When someone really loves you, it fills you up from the inside the way incense fills up a room. It is a light in the darkness. Did you know that you and I can love others, even when they don't love us? God gives us that power. He wants us to spread the fragrance of love, through the Holy Spirit, into the lives of other people. So many people tell me that they just can't witness, but I know that's not true. Every Christian can be a great witness. We all have the ability to spread love and spread the message of God, acting as a beautiful fragrance that permeates a room.

Jesus told us to share the fruits of the Spirit: love, joy, peace, patience, kindness, goodness, faithfulness, gentleness, and self-control. Compared to eternity, we are on this earth such a short time—why would you want to share anything *but* those things? Kindness, joy, patience, love—these are all things that can permeate a room. Isn't that the kind of room you want to be in?

Evangelism

-32-

Fishers of Men

Object:
A fishing pole, line, and hook

Scripture:

When Jesus heard that John had been put in prison, he returned to Galilee. Leaving Nazareth, he went and lived in Capernaum, which was by the lake in the area of Zebulun and Naphtali— to fulfill what was said through the prophet Isaiah: "Land of Zebulun and land of Naphtali, the way to the sea, along with the Jordan, Galilee of the Gentiles— the people living in darkness have seen a great light; on those living in the land of the shadow of death a light has dawned." From that time on Jesus began to preach, "Repent, for the kingdom of heaven is near."

—*Matthew 4:12–17*

A little boy was fishing with his father at a quiet stream one day. He had a basket full of fish, while a man nearby hadn't had a bite all day. He asked the boy, "What's your secret?" The little boy mumbled, "You have to keep the worms warm."

Ask a group of seasoned fishers for tips, and they will all give you a different answer. There are some basics, though, for every fisher. To catch a fish you need a pole, a line, a hook, and what else? Of course you have to go where the fish are—a lake, a stream, or an ocean. You also need bait—something to get the attention of the fish and make them bite. Finally, the most important thing is to get the hook in the water and hope that there are fish where you are fishing.

But what about fishing for people? Humans need stronger bait than fish, so you need something attractive enough that people will come and see what you've got—and that they want. You've also got to *go* to the people.

Jesus tells us that He will give us power—Holy Spirit power. When He comes into our lives and abides in us, that is the real motivating force behind us; it is that love that helps us to go out and love others. When people observe this loving, caring, unselfish spirit in us, they will want it for themselves. That's the bait.

A college football player was a camp counselor at a YMCA camp. One week he had some kids from the inner city who were particularly tough. One of the kids played tricks on the guy almost every day; he put cracker crumbs in his bed, short-sheeted him—just to name a few things. But the counselor never raised his voice. Instead, he loved the kid even more. The last night at the camp, they were going down to the campfire. The little kid walked quietly by the counselor's side, slid his tiny hand into that of the counselor's, and walked silently alongside him. Finally, he asked, "Is Jesus like you?"

It's easy enough to go where the fish are. Now ask yourself if you're offering truly tempting bait.

-33-

Spreading the Good News

Object:
A dusty book

Scripture:

For it is with your heart that you believe and are justified, and it is with your mouth that you confess and are saved. As the Scripture says, "Anyone who trusts in Him will never be put to shame. For there is no difference between Jew and Gentile—the same Lord is Lord of all and richly blesses all who call on Him, for, "Everyone who calls on the name of the Lord will be saved." How, then, can they call on the one they have not believed in? And how can they believe in the one of whom they have not heard? And how can they hear without someone preaching to them? And how can they preach unless they are sent? As it is written, "How beautiful are the feet of those who bring good news!" But not all the Israelites accepted the good news. For Isaiah says, "Lord, who has believed our message?" Consequently, faith comes from hearing the message, and the message is heard through the word of Christ.

—Romans 10:10–17

Imagine walking into an enormous room. The ceilings are higher than any other, the lights are dim, and every wall in the room is packed with rows and rows of books. Books about history, science, architecture, art—some of the world's most important knowledge is in this room. But the books are very dusty, as though none of them have been opened in years. With such a wealth of information, wouldn't you wonder why no one is interested in sharing it?

We've got an important book, one that certainly doesn't deserve to be collecting dust on a shelf somewhere. The Bible has a formula for world peace and brotherhood, but we have to actually read it. For it is by seeing through the word that we come to believe, and by believing that we have life.

Because external (worldly) things give man the feeling of satisfying only his own wants, we must change man from the inside, not the outside. How do we do that? We have a formula written for us in the Bible. There are an overwhelming number of verses in the Bible referring to evangelism, so this is no small undertaking for us. It is our duty as Christians to make disciples, but how would we know what to do if we never read it ourselves? If someone were to ask you about Jesus's miracles, could you name one? If you told someone to read John 3:16, could you tell him what it said?

So next time you read from your Bible, take a few notes. Then lend it to a friend. Take every opportunity to share this important message; it will never be heard if it's not read first.

-34-

The Weakest Link

Object:
A chain

Scripture:

Live in harmony with one another. Do not be proud, but be willing to associate with people of low position. Do not be conceited. Do not repay anyone evil for evil. Be careful to do what is right in the eyes of everybody. If it is possible, as far as it depends on you, live at peace with everyone. . . . If your enemy is hungry, feed him; if he is thirsty, give him something to drink. . . . Do not be overcome by evil, but overcome evil with good."
—Romans 12:16–21

How do you feel when you think of a chain? Do you think of a prisoner in shackles? Do you think of tire chains? Jewelry? Keychains? Whatever chain you think of, that chain is meant to be strong and sturdy, made of many little links that will ultimately connect one thing to something else. But what happens if one of those links goes missing? The chain no longer works—a prisoner could escape, your favorite bracelet could fall off your wrist, or your car could slide on the ice. All because of one little link.

As Christians we are created independently, but we are meant to link together with other Christians. The more we connect, the more we build each other up. When we live in harmony, pray together, worship together, cry together, work together, and generally live in fellowship, we create a stronger chain. The stronger the chain, the harder it is to break.

Have you ever heard the saying, "A chain is only as strong as its weakest link"?

It's also important to frequently add new links to God's chain. A family we knew years ago moved to Minneapolis, because the husband, an engineer, got a job in construction. They had a young son, John, who played often with the neighbor's little boy in the backyard. One day, the neighbor asked little John, "Where do you go to Sunday school?" John answered, "Oh I don't go." The neighbor asked, "Would you like to come with me?" With that one question, the entire family began going to church.

That boy is one link in the chain, and he was not afraid to add to it. Are you a weak link, or are you adding to God's chain? If you're nervous, start small. Bring your Bible to a public place (a park or coffee shop) and read; maybe you'll get someone's attention. Casually mention to a friend something that resonated in last week's sermon. Invite that friend to come with you next week. The stronger the chain, the heavier the load it can bear. But a chain with a link missing? You might as well use a string.

-35-

The Salt of the Earth

Object:
A salt shaker

Scripture:

You are the salt of the earth. But if the salt loses its saltiness, how can it be made salty again? It is no longer good for anything, except to be thrown out and trampled by men.

—Matthew 5:13

With all the different flavorings out there, sometimes it's difficult to know the right thing to use to spice up a dish. Cinnamon? Cumin? Coriander? Sometimes you just go back to the basics. Salt is one of those flavorings that takes just a little bit to make a huge difference. It blends into the whole dish, and you can't see it, but the taste is improved so much that you know it's there!

Christians are a lot like salt; they are the flavoring of society. You need to add only a little bit, and it makes everything so much better. God wants us to go everywhere, to all parts of society, all over the world. You couldn't pick the Christians out of society just by looking, but you know they're there because, like a soup with a touch of salt, the whole has been improved.

Has anyone ever told you, "You're the salt of the earth"? Do you know the origin of that phrase? It was first used around AD 30, when Jesus was giving His Sermon on the Mount; here He preached many of His moral lessons to His disciples and a large crowd. Referring to the crowd as "salt" was a compliment, because in those days salt was used as both currency and as a preservative. He told them they were very important people, yes, but He also said they had live up to it.

Salt of the earth? How do we do we live up to that standard? Like salt in a shaker, Christians have our own little shaker—the church. When we're not doing enough, God lets us know—He shakes us up a little, spreads us out. That's when we have work to do. In Paul's letter to the Ephesians, he says, "For we are God's workmanship, created in Christ Jesus to do good works, which God prepared in advance for us to do." Missionaries are in all parts of the world—Guatemala, South Africa, Niger— spreading God's message one small act at a time.

But you don't have to travel farther than your own neighborhood to be the salt of the earth. Help an elderly woman cross the street. Give a little boy a dollar to buy a treat (just imagine how his face will light up!). Offer to babysit for the busiest couple you know. Bake banana bread for your best friend just to say how much she means to you. Invite your neighbor to church if he's alone on a Sunday morning. Though they may seem insignificant to the person who does them, all of these small acts could mean the world to the receiver of the action. Are you adding any flavor to the world?

-36-

Where It All Begins

Object:
A roll of film

Scripture:

But you will receive power when the Holy Spirit comes on you; and you will be my witnesses in Jerusalem, and in all Judea and Samaria, and to the ends of the earth.

—Acts 1:8

Have you ever seen a photograph that truly moved you? Perhaps it was the sun setting over a quiet mountain lake. Your daughter excitedly blowing out the candles at her first birthday. A man and woman sharing their first dance as a married couple, gazing contentedly into each other's eyes.

These photographs don't appear like magic; a series of important steps must happen to capture these special moments. You snap the picture. Film is removed in a dark room. It is then placed in a developing solution for a certain amount of time, with things like temperature and the speed of the film taken into account. Next the film is placed into a hypo solution, then washed. Finally, that perfect photograph comes to you.

When I was in the service, I was stationed way up north for some time. It was very picturesque: we had dog sleds, snow-mobiles, boats, rafts, mountains, everything you can imagine when you think of the arctic. I thought I'd capitalize on this by taking photos and selling them, so I bought books, equipment, chemicals—the works. The books explained everything I needed to know: temperature, focus, range, cropping, aperture, etc. The problem? I knew all the advanced techniques, but I didn't know where to begin. I knew steps two, three, and four, but not step one. I needed someone to explain the basics of photography to me: How do I turn the camera on? What do I press to take the picture?

Spiritually speaking, we have all sorts of equipment—theological and dogmatic. We have discussed theological issues backwards and forwards. But the world is still a mess, full of hatred and tension. We have all the equipment for peace, and we have the desire, but we don't know where to begin.

One person can do huge things. Back in the 1950s, Dr. Bill Bright started a revolution in his small apartment in Berkeley, California. He had been hoping to reach out to the dispossessed people in his area, but he found that there were a number of organizations already vying to help them. So he turned to college students instead, and he found that this was an open field. Beginning with just a few students in his living room, he started what would eventually become Campus Crusade for Christ. A few years later, he started a movement called the Lay Institute for Evangelism, which is home to thousands of workers every year. Both of these successes demonstrate what the faith and determination of one person can bring about.

Bill Bright started in his living room. Where will you start?

-37-

The Inner Man

Object:
A peanut

Scripture:

I became a servant of this gospel by the gift of God's grace given me through the working of His power. Although I am less than the least of all God's people, this grace was given me: to preach to the Gentiles the unsearchable riches of Christ, and to make plain to everyone the administration of this mystery, which for ages past was kept hidden in God, who created all things.

—*Ephesians 3:7–9*

Have you ever sat in the bleachers at a baseball game? As you scooted down the row to your seat, you probably heard the crunching of peanut shells under your feet. They're a staple for the American pastime—it's almost as common to eat peanuts as it is to do the seventh inning stretch. Eating peanuts can be kind of a hassle, though—you really have to commit yourself to breaking those shells to get through to the sweet center!

A nut can give life in two ways: First, it can be eaten right away and serve as tasty, salty food for someone. Alternatively, it can be planted; in that case the person has to wait until it produces a new crop. (A peanut takes just one season, but a walnut takes years.) When that nut is planted in the ground, it takes a long time for the little tiny bacteria in the soil to finally eat away the shell so it can start a new plant. The conditions need to be just right for that life within the shell to burst forth.

We are like nuts in many ways. We can give love and energy to others right away—kind of like nourishment. It is always a great thing to be kind and loving to others. Or, we can die to ourselves, take root, and produce other Christians so that the Church will grow and grow. In both cases, we have to break out of our shells.

In this scripture, a secret was finally revealed to Jesus's followers. This was no mystery, like a detective story. The Holy Spirit revealed that God was not to be the property of a nation or a people, but of the whole world. Paul told the Gentiles that, "through the gospel the Gentiles are heirs together with Israel, members together of one body, and sharers together in the promise in Christ Jesus"; this was a new insight not shared with earlier generations. Armed now with this information, what were they supposed to do? The intent now was that the "manifold wisdom of God" should be made known. They needed to break out of their shells to do that.

You have a directive: to spread God's message. Just like you can't eat a peanut without first breaking the shell, no one will hear your message if you keep it to yourself.

-38-

Spread the Word

Object:
Yeast

Scripture:

For the word of God is living and active. Sharper than any double-edged sword, it penetrates even to dividing soul and spirit, joints and marrow; it judges the thoughts and attitudes of the heart.

—*Hebrews 4:12*

Have you ever baked homemade bread? If so, your first reaction is probably to remember fondly that delicious smell that permeated throughout your house. You may also be familiar with yeast, a basic requirement for baking bread. It only takes a little yeast to make the other ingredients—flour, water, shortening, and sugar—rise. This process is calling "budding": one cell becomes two, and two become four, and four become eight, and so on.

Our Lord tells us that we must be like yeast, sharing our faith with others. One Christian becomes two, two becomes four, four becomes eight, and so on. Eventually, there will be enough of us spreading good news that we can suppress the overwhelming messages of hate we hear all the time.

When we say "word" it could mean a lot of different things. We all speak words, but they are meaningless to someone who speaks a different language. If I say, "Can I borrow some sugar?" to my new neighbor from Spain, I might be met with a blank stare. If I say, "¿Puedo pedir prestado un poco de azúcar?" then my neighbor might actually give me a bowl of sugar so that I can bake my cake. Different cultures have a greater number of words for different things, depending on how they live and what is important.

What if I spoke a little Greek? "Un archai en ho logos": In the beginning was the Word. To Lutherans, the Bible is the inspired Word of God. We believe the original manuscript is without error, truly God's message to mankind. The Bible is one of the means of grace, and the two sacraments are based on the Word. This inspired Word is twofold: it contains law and gospel. The law describes the works and obedience required of us. The gospel tells a message of God's love and forgiveness, along with the good news of salvation.

Words can hurt and help, destroy or build up, heal or make sick. Don Gossett wrote a book called *What You Say Is What You Get*. His goal is to empower his readers to use the Word of God to change their lives. Are you sharing God's Word with others? Are you spreading a message of hope and joy? If what you say is what you get, think about what you want to get back.

-39-

Who is an Evangelist?

Object:
A postage stamp

Scripture:

When a Samaritan woman came to draw water, Jesus said to her, "Will you give me a drink?" . . . The Samaritan woman said to him, "You are a Jew and I am a Samaritan woman. How can you ask me for a drink?" (For Jews do not associate with Samaritans.) Jesus answered her, "If you knew the gift of God and who it is that asks you for a drink, you would have asked him and he would have given you living water." "Sir," the woman said, "you have nothing to draw with and the well is deep. Where can you get this living water?" . . . Jesus answered, "Everyone who drinks this water will be thirsty again, but whoever drinks the water I give him will never thirst. Indeed, the water I give him will become in him a spring of water welling up to eternal life." The woman said to him, "Sir, give me this water so that I won't get thirsty and have to keep coming here to draw water." . . . Jesus declared, "Believe me, woman, a time is coming when you will worship the Father neither on this mountain nor in Jerusalem. You Samaritans worship what you do not know; we worship what we do know, for salvation is from the Jews. Yet a time is coming and has now come when the true worshipers will worship the Father in spirit and truth, for they are the kind of worshipers the Father seeks. God is spirit, and His worshipers must worship in spirit and in truth." . . . The woman said, "I know that Messiah is coming."

—*John 4:7–25*

We've all used a stamp before. Maybe you had a pen pal when you were young, so you used stamps to mail letters to your friend. Maybe you're a stamp collector, and you've got a few rare and valuable ones. Maybe you just use stamps to mail your bills every month. A stamp does a lot of things: It has to stick to the letter, otherwise the receiver must pay the postage. It's nice looking, bearing the image of flags, flowers, events, or famous people. It takes a licking from the sender. Finally, a stamp doesn't mind getting smeared; sometimes by the time you receive a letter, it has been postmarked so many times you can't even see the stamp anymore!

We're a lot like a stamp. We have to stick to our important job of being a Christian. Sometimes, when life throws curveballs our way, we really take a licking (but with God's assistance we always make it to our destination). And as Christians, we bear the seal of He who sends us, Jesus Christ.

Jesus gave us a commandment: "Go into all the world, make disciples of all nations!" The way we do that is through evangelism. So what exactly is an evangelist? The word has two parts: *eu* meaning "good" and *angel* meaning "messenger of God." So an evangelist is a good messenger of God. Put simply, it is someone who tells the good news of God's salvation through Jesus Christ. In our story from John, Jesus reached out to a Samaritan woman even though Jews and Samaritans didn't typically associate. To an evangelist, there is no one who is unworthy of hearing the good news.

In the same way that a letter will not travel anywhere without a stamp, we have an important message about God's love, and we need to deliver it.

-40-

How Beautiful Are the Feet

Object:
A pair of shoes

Scripture:
While they were still talking about this, Jesus Himself stood among them and said to them, "Peace be with you." They were startled and frightened, thinking they saw a ghost. He said to them, "Why are you troubled, and why do doubts rise in your minds? Look at my hands and my feet. It is I myself! Touch me and see; a ghost does not have flesh and bones, as you see I have." When He had said this, He showed them His hands and feet. And while they still did not believe it because of joy and amazement, He asked them, "Do you have anything here to eat?" They gave Him a piece of broiled fish, and He took it and ate it in their presence. He said to them, "This is what I told you while I was still with you: Everything must be fulfilled that is written about me in the Law of Moses, the Prophets and the Psalms."
—Luke 24:36–44

Imagine walking into a shoe store, where you see rows and rows of shoes for every occasion: walking shoes, dancing shoes, dress shoes, climbing shoes, penny loafers, platform heels, hiking boots, stilettos, ballet flats, sandals, and shoes for every particular sport. There are big ones, little ones, narrow ones, wide ones—shoes to fit all manner and ages of people. It can get a little overwhelming to pick one!

No matter what you end up putting on your feet, however, that shoe was designed with a specific purpose in mind. Shoes were designed so that people could move and work and dance and play and walk and run and any number of things.

People are just like that: we are all very different—young, old, small, large, plain, fancy—but we all have a very important purpose. So where exactly are we going? Where are the feet taking the shoes? (It's not the shoes leading the feet!)

Two thousand years ago, Paul said, "How beautiful are the feet of those who bring good news!" All over the world, there is sorrow, despair, and misery. But we have an uplifting message—the good news of eternal life—and we need to share it. Imagine spending your entire life poor and despondent, unsure of how to better your situation. Now imagine someone taking the time to share God's message. What a difference!

In our nation we have a "get up and go" philosophy. Our nation was founded on the principle that we should make something of ourselves, that we should not sit around and wait for something to happen. Today we have Americans traveling to every corner of the world making things happen—starting businesses and doing world-changing research. Doing is almost a cult in America.

Christian singer Mark Schultz describes perfectly this concept of going, going, going: "I can't stand still, can I get a witness? . . . I think I'm running just to catch myself." It's one thing to be moving constantly if you're doing God's work. It's another to be running yourself into the ground, wasting time. Think about how you spend your time, about the shoes that you're wearing. Are you spreading God's Word, leaving His footprints behind you wherever you go?

-41-

Seeds of Love

Object:
Seeds

Scripture:

Then Jesus came to them and said, "All authority in heaven and on earth has been given to me. Therefore go and make disciples of all nations, baptizing them in the name of the Father and of the Son and of the Holy Spirit, and teaching them to obey everything I have commanded you. And surely I am with you always, to the very end of the age.

—Matthew 28:18–20

If you plant a grape seed, what will grow from it? When dandelion seeds float through the wind and land on the ground, what do you get?

The Bible is very clear that we reap what we sow. Galatians 6:8 says, "The one who sows to please his sinful nature, from that nature will reap destruction; the one who sows to please the Spirit, from the Spirit will reap eternal life." Do you want to spread hate around the world, getting hate and bitterness back? Or would you rather plant seeds of love?

The answer is easy. But what exactly does it mean to plant seeds of love? A dark, bitter person probably could not do this no matter how hard he tried. Someone who abides in Christ, on the other hand, can do it without even trying. According to the Bible, if we abide in Christ, and Him in us, then we naturally do what He wants with our lives, performing great works and deeds all based on the love of God within us. Our lives are dynamic and full, and that love naturally exudes from us the way a cup overflows when it is full. And love isn't the only thing we can pass on. The fruits of the Spirit are love, joy, peace, patience, kindness, goodness, faithfulness, gentleness, and self-control. When we abide in Christ, we exude all of these things.

Let's take a look at our scripture. Matthew, called Levi, had just become a disciple of Christ. These last verses of Matthew state three things: Jesus made an important assertion, saying all authority on Heaven and Earth had been given to Him. He then gave an assignment to His followers, commanding them to go and make disciples of all nations. Finally, He gave them assurance, saying "I am with you always."

For Jesus's followers, that was a pretty big assignment to get directly from the Christ Himself. Do you think they thought to themselves, *Well, what now? How do I go about "making disciples"?*

His followers took the assignment seriously, and we are to do the same. We have an important duty as Christians to spread God's Word, and we can do this in two ways. We can tell people explicitly—can you quote John 3:16? The other way is plant seeds of love, joy, peace, patience, kindness, goodness, faithfulness, gentleness, and self-control. That way, when people see you they will want what you have.

But that can work the other way too. Think twice before you zip by another driver to steal a parking space; that driver might look at the icthus sticker on your car and be turned off! There's a quote that says, "Be careful of the life you lead, for sometimes you are the only Bible people read." Are you planting seeds that will produce fruit?

Faith

-42-

The Heart of Understanding

Object:
A flower and a cookie

Scripture:

That same day two of them were going to a village called Emmaus. . . . Jesus himself came up and walked along with them; but they were kept from recognizing him. He asked them, "What are you discussing together as you walk along?" They stood still, their faces downcast. One of them . . . asked Him, "Are you only a visitor to Jerusalem and do not know the things that have happened there in these days?" "What things?" He asked. "About Jesus of Nazareth," they replied. "He was a prophet, powerful in word and deed before God and all the people. The chief priests and our rulers handed Him over to be sentenced to death, and they crucified Him; but we had hoped that He was the one who was going to redeem Israel. And what is more, it is the third day since all this took place. In addition, some of our women . . . went to the tomb early this morning but didn't find His body. They came and told us that they had seen a vision of angels, who said He was alive. Then some of our companions went to the tomb and found it just as the women had said, but Him they did not see." He said to them, "How foolish you are, and how slow of heart to believe all that the prophets have spoken! Did not the Christ have to suffer these

*things and then enter His glory?" . . . As they approached the village to
which they were going, . . . they urged Him strongly, "Stay with us, for it
is nearly evening; . . ." So He went in to stay with them. When He was
at the table with them, He took bread, gave thanks, broke it, and began to
give it to them. Then their eyes were opened and they recognized Him, and
He disappeared from their sight. They asked each other, "Were not our
hearts burning within us while He talked with us on the road and opened
the Scriptures to us?" They got up and returned at once to Jerusalem. . . .
Then the two told what had happened on the way, and how Jesus was
recognized by them when He broke the bread.*

—Luke 24:13–35

Some of you may remember learning about Hull House, the
late-nineteenth century settlement house on South Halstad in
the slums of Chicago. What you may not have learned about
is the founder, Jane Addams, who lived to serve others. She
helped the recently arrived European immigrants—most of
whom were poor. She offered speech classes, drama classes,
and cooking classes, doing everything she could to help them
assimilate. With her fame spreading, a reporter asked her
why she wanted to live this way; she told him to meet her at
the building with some flowers and cookies and she'd show
him. She went out into the street on a cold October day and
offered a cookie *or* a flower to each child on the street. All of
the flowers were gone before a single cookie was touched.
Her point? She was there to bring just a little beauty into
otherwise drab lives.

Children are fascinating for many reasons. A tiny baby
can recognize love; in fact, hundreds of studies show that
there is prenatal learning. That can be good and bad: babies
in the womb can take in positive feelings of love, peace, and
contentment, but they can also learn tension, conflict, and

neglect. A child mistreated in the womb may resent its mother for years.

Remember when you were a kid and you could spend hours just flying a kite, without a care in the world? Perhaps you spent hours playing Ring around the Rosie, oblivious of what the game meant because you were having such fun. Robert Fulghum wrote a book called *All I Really Need to Know I Learned in Kindergarten.* Credos from "share everything" to "hold hands and stick together" are basics for life, and sometimes we get so caught-up in grown-up business that we forget about kindness, imagination, and hope. It took a miracle—the reappearance of Jesus—to remind the men on the road to Emmaus what hope was.

What will it take to remind you?

-43-

Small Stuff!

Object:
A mustard seed

Scripture:

And Jesus answered them, "Have faith in God. Truly, I say to you, whoever says to this mountain, 'Be taken up and thrown into the sea,' and does not doubt in his heart, but believes that what he says will come to pass, it will be done for him. Therefore I tell you, whatever you ask in prayer, believe that you have received it, and it will be yours.

—Mark 11:22–25

Mustard seeds are among the smallest of seeds. Small, yellow, and perfectly round, they are cultivated all over the world and used in cooking. Jesus tells us that if we have faith as large as a mustard seed, "we can say to this mountain, move and it will be cast into the sea. For with God, nothing is impossible." That says a lot about a little bit of faith!

Every one of us is created in the image of God. We can choose to be overwhelmed by our insignificance next to God, or we can believe what Jesus said—that a little faith moves mountains. Sometimes we have to make that choice when we feel very small: even when we are having a hard time, even when we believe the outlook is hopeless, a little faith will go a long way.

God has a plan for our lives, but we have to accept it. This is a true story about a little girl in Philadelphia, Pennsylvania. She was sobbing outside a church when she was turned away because there was no room for her. The pastor saw her as he walked by and she told him, "I can't go to Sunday school." She was poorly dressed, and he guessed that was why she was turned away. Still, he took her by the hand and found a place for her in the class. Two years later she was found dead in one of the poor tenement buildings, and the parents called the kind pastor to handle the funeral arrangements. As her little body was moved, they noticed a worn, crumpled purse—one she must have found in a dumpster at some point. Inside the purse was fifty-seven cents and a note in her childlike handwriting that read, "This is to help build the church a little bigger so more children can go to Sunday school."

She had saved this money for two years as an offering of love.

The pastor took the money, and the next Sunday he challenged his deacons to get busy raising money for a larger building. A newspaper published the story, a realtor offered them a lot, a check came in, and in five years they had raised over $250,000. Today, Temple Baptist Church has a seating capacity of 3,300, and the Good Samaritan Hospital came soon after.

It all started with a child's loving gift of fifty-seven cents.

Remember, it is not the size of the gift that matters, but when you give from your heart, great things can happen.

-44-

Have a Little Faith

Object:
A blank check

Scripture:

Leaving that place, Jesus withdrew to the region of Tyre and Sidon. A Canaanite woman from that vicinity came to him, crying out, "Lord, Son of David, have mercy on me! My daughter is suffering terribly from demon-possession." Jesus did not answer a word. So his disciples came to Him and urged Him, "Send her away, for she keeps crying out after us." He answered, "I was sent only to the lost sheep of Israel." The woman came and knelt before Him. "Lord, help me!" she said. He replied, "It is not right to take the children's bread and toss it to their dogs." "Yes, Lord," she said, "but even the dogs eat the crumbs that fall from their masters' table." Then Jesus answered, "Woman, you have great faith! Your request is granted." And her daughter was healed from that very hour.

—Matthew 15:21–28

What was one of the first rules you learned about writing checks? You learned to write the date, to sign it, to fill in the memo line, and to add the transaction to your check register. What else? You have to fill in the amount! I was always told not to write a blank check, because anyone could find it and cash it for a huge sum. You'd be really disappointed in yourself if that happened! Still, some people do write them. A check with nothing but a signature on it represents a leap of faith in two ways. The check giver has faith that the receiver will not overspend. The receiver of the check, in turn, has faith in the giver's integrity—that the check won't bounce.

Today we are a society based on credit, which requires great faith in others. Bankers, realtors, car dealers, and friends and family make promises to one another on a daily basis, and we are all taken on our word. You may not realize it, but in many of your day-to-day transactions, you are putting serious trust in other people. You trust your doctor to give you sound advice regarding your health. You trust your bank to guard your most valued possessions. You trust your waiter not to run off with your credit card. You trust your therapist not to share your most intimate secrets. In all of these situations, you're turning over two very valuable things—your life and your money—to complete strangers.

Considering how much credit we give to each other, do you have that much faith in God? The woman in our scripture did. As a Canaanite, she was an outsider to the disciples, and they carried a deep prejudice toward her. It didn't matter that her child was suffering. "Send her away!" they cried, not wanting her to bother Jesus. But she didn't waver, even when Jesus himself appeared to refuse her. Why did Matthew tell this story? He wanted to illustrate the new covenant: a woman, not a man came to Jesus for healing. And even though she was a Canaanite—an enemy of the Jews—Jesus rewarded her because she had strong faith.

We are rewarded for our faith as well. It's easiest during times of smooth sailing, but ask yourself: would your faith hold up under pressure?

-45-

Your Victory!

Object:
A big V on a piece of cardboard

Scripture:

So do not throw away your confidence; it will be richly rewarded. You need to persevere so that when you have done the will of God, you will receive what he has promised. For in just a very little while, "He who is coming will come and will not delay. But my righteous one will live by faith. And if he shrinks back, I will not be pleased with him."

—Hebrews 10:35–38

V for Victory is an old symbol. Winston Churchill used it extensively during World War II to motivate the Allies. Remember the crowds of people celebrating in the streets when the war was over? Many of them were holding signs like this one. Since the end of the war, Europeans have commemorated the German and Japanese surrenders with V-E Day and V-J Day. This symbol is so powerful because it has dual meaning: it represents both the motivation during battle and also the victory itself.

Victory begins with an individual conviction; it demands personal commitment to a goal. Eventually, the idea spreads to others, like a domino effect. Have you ever been to a sporting event and seen the crowd do "the wave"? Motivation to win spreads a lot like that.

Victory to the Christian means overcoming evil: the conquering of sin and death. Christ achieved that victory, and now, because of his sacrifice, we have the means to do so as well. Acknowledging this, we fight an individual battle; however, when we add up the individual battles, we understand that we have won the larger war by creating a world of peace and brotherhood. Remember this begins in the heart of each person.

The first step is a confrontation with God. In our scripture, God warns the men to be brave when things get difficult. In the passage before, He was admonishing them, reminding them of how when they first received the light, they stood their ground in the face of suffering. They were persecuted and insulted, and their property was confiscated, but they remained strong because they knew they had a lasting possession in God. "It is a dreadful thing to fall into the hands of the living God," He scolds them, warning of what will happen if they lose faith.

So here we have God answering the question asked of Jesus: "What must I do to inherit life?" If there is to be any victory of the church, the individual must respond with faith, bravery, and determination. The individual is the heart of the movement.

Think back to our example. Wars produce all kinds of heroes: generals, captains, prime ministers. What does it take to deactivate a ticking bomb? What does it take to lead a group of soldiers into battle, knowing you're in the line of fire? For these men and women, a little faith goes a long way—faith that they are doing the right thing, faith that someone is watching out for them. They come home heroes to people thankful for their bravery. What is your greatest victory?

-46-

The Keys of the Kingdom

Object:
A pair of keys

Scripture:

Jesus . . . asked his disciples, "Who do people say the Son of Man is?" They replied, "Some say John the Baptist; others say Elijah; and still others, Jeremiah or one of the prophets." "But what about you?" he asked. "Who do you say I am?" Simon Peter answered, "You are the Christ, the Son of the living God." Jesus replied, "Blessed are you, Simon son of Jonah, for this was not revealed to you by man, but by my Father in heaven. And I tell you that you are Peter, and on this rock I will build my church, and the gates of Hades will not overcome it. I will give you the keys of the kingdom of heaven; whatever you bind on earth will be bound in heaven, and whatever you loose on earth will be loosed in heaven."

—Matthew 16:13–19

What was the first key you ever used? Did you have a key to lock up your first bicycle? What about your locker at school? We've all used keys at some point. You've used them to lock your house, your car, or a safe deposit box. Some keys are intangible, like the key to good health, the key to your future, or the key to a better golf game.

Many religions claim they have the key to Heaven. Jesus, however, was the only one who ever said, "I came down from Heaven. I am the Way." He told us directly that He would give us the keys to Heaven. That's a key you don't want to lose!

If you were walking down the street and a man shouted from a second story window, "Help! Fire!" would you just keep on strolling along, pretending not to notice? Of course not. You would run for help, call 9-1-1, maybe even get a ladder and attempt to help him yourself.

We need to apply this same sense of urgency to our spiritual lives. Many of us find ourselves thinking of the eternal, of life and death. "What happens when I die?" is one of the most age-old questions of mankind. Maybe a life-threatening operation instigates this thinking—a sleepless night, waiting through the oppressing darkness for the light of morning. All along, we're searching for the key to eternal life. We're spiritually dying, yet we don't cry out for help. We're cut off from God, rendered blind. We don't realize we have the keys in our hand.

So what *is* the key to the kingdom of Heaven? Jesus said again and again that all we have to do to gain eternal life is believe in Him. The key is faith. It was not Peter who was a rock, it was his steadfast faith.

Jesus said, "Here I am! I stand at the door and knock. If anyone hears my voice and opens the door, I will come in and eat with him, and he with me." We have the right key, and we know which door it opens. What are you waiting for?

-47-

Heroes

Object:
A slingshot

Scripture:

I can do everything through him who gives me strength.

—Philippians 4:13

Did you ever use a slingshot when you were a kid? It was kind of a deviant thing—to pick up a rock and send it flying through the air at something (or someone) unsuspecting. Maybe you never used one. Maybe to you, a slingshot just represents one of the great underdog stories: David beating Goliath.

The David and Goliath story is a truly inspirational one. We've all heard it at some point. Sunday school teachers and preachers tell it to their students and congregations, parents tell it to their kids, coaches use it to encourage their players, and speakers use it to motivate their audiences. All of this talk is about one boy who had faith that God would help him defeat a monster.

This story is so affecting because it demonstrates that one person can do a lot if he or she simply has a little faith. It reminds me of a story I heard about a little boy who got stung by a jellyfish when he was out on a raft. Though his family was nearby, he was on the raft alone and didn't know what to do. So he prayed. His family saw him struggling and swam to his aid. That could have been a terrifying experience, but faith got him through it.

The Old Testament is full of heroes. Moses was enjoying a simple life in Midian with his wife and father-in-law. The people of Israel were suffering, but Moses didn't have a care in the world. But God had bigger plans for him. "Come," God said to him from a burning bush, "I will send you to pharaoh to bring my people out." Moses argued with him, unsure whether or not people would believe God sent him. Finally, he stepped up to the challenge, eventually performing miracles that would influence Jewish thought for the next three thousand years.

Gideon, a judge, was another hero. While preparing for battle, God helped Gideon understand His true greatness. With only three hundred soldiers, Gideon defeated the Midianites.

You may be familiar with the story of Shadrach, Meshach, and Abednego. (This story has been represented many times in music and film.) The three men were brought to the court of King Nebuchadnezzar II and asked to bow down to a monument of him. When they refused to worship this false idol, they were thrown in a fiery furnace. The king ordered the flames turned up seven times hotter than normal, and they watched expectantly. Instead of the three men burning, however, they saw four men walking around in the fire. The Son of God was in there with them, protecting his faithful servants.

These stories teach us that anyone, with a little faith, can be a hero. When you help an elderly woman cross the street, you may be a hero to her. If you buy a new Bible for a friend, he might view that as heroic. And when you continue to pray, in the face of adversity, you will come out stronger on the other side.

Many years ago, an issue of *U.S. News and World Report* surveyed people, asking them who their heroes were. The number one answer? Jesus Christ. He taught us what it takes to be a hero. It's time to pick up the slingshot.

-48-

The Long Road

Object:
An annual plant and a perennial plant

Scripture:

I have fought the good fight, I have finished the race, I have kept the faith. Now there is in store for me the crown of righteousness, which the Lord, the righteous Judge, will award to me on that day—and not only to me, but also to all who have longed for his appearing. . . . At my first defense, no one came to my support, but everyone deserted me. . . . But the Lord stood at my side and gave me strength, so that through me the message might be fully proclaimed and all the Gentiles might hear it. And I was delivered from the lion's mouth. The Lord will rescue me from every evil attack and will bring me safely to His heavenly kingdom. To Him be glory for ever and ever.
—2 Timothy 4:6–8, 16–18

Have you ever seen it snow in the springtime? Beautiful flowers are blooming everywhere; one minute it's bright and colorful, and the next all of the blooms are covered in a blanket of snow. The sight is a bit puzzling.

An annual plant is just what the name implies: it has life for just one year. it begins the year as a tiny bud, it blooms,

113

and then it dies when the frost hits. To get a new one, you have to plant a new seed. The perennial plant only appears to die when the frost hits. It lies dormant during the cold winter, but because it has life deep down in its rootstock, it blooms again when the spring comes and the rain softens the ground. Each time around, it comes back stronger than the year before.

Some Christians are like the annual plant: when the climate around them turns cold, they die. Even when their surroundings warm up again, they do not rise to new life. Other Christians are more like the perennial plant (a dahlia or red valerian, perhaps). These Christians appear to die when their environment turns cold and hostile, but the instant warmth and light touch them, they rise again, stronger than before. We need to establish this kind of life cycle, so that new Christians can grow from the seeds we plant.

From here I would like to point out the importance of perspective: long-term versus short-term. Two men—Paul and Martin Luther King Jr.—illustrate this in historical context.

Paul viewed the road to salvation from the long-term perspective. In his early years, when he was a strict Jew, he was lost. God had to enter his life boldly, physically blinding him on the way to Damascus, in order to get him to finally see spiritually. He could have been angry, but instead he proclaimed the greatness of God for standing by him and giving him the strength to proclaim the Gospel.

King, a Baptist minister, also accomplished great things because he had great perspective. Though he was persecuted early in his career, he saw that what he was doing would lead to great change; he went on to become the youngest person ever to receive the Nobel Peace Prize for his dedication to the Civil Rights Movement.

Both of these men demonstrate the importance of having long-term perspective in the face of adversity. It's easy to wither away, like the annual plant, when your environment turns hostile. Like the perennial plant, however, the world's greatest leaders have faced hardship again and again, emerging victorious each time. As a Christian, you know where to go for shelter when your environment turns hostile. Will you come back stronger?

-49-

Take Ahold of Life

Object:
A microscope

Scripture:

There was a rich man . . . who lived in luxury every day. At his gate was laid a beggar named Lazarus, covered with sores and longing to eat what fell from the rich man's table. . . . The time came when the beggar died and the angels carried him to Abraham's side. The rich man also died and was buried. In hell, where he was in torment, he looked up and saw Abraham far away, with Lazarus by his side. So he called to him, "Father Abraham, have pity on me and send Lazarus to dip the tip of his finger in water and cool my tongue, because I am in agony in this fire." But Abraham replied, "Son, remember that in your lifetime you received your good things, while Lazarus received bad things, but now he is comforted here and you are in agony. And besides all this, between us and you a great chasm has been fixed, so that those who want to go from here to you cannot, nor can anyone cross over from there to us." He answered, "Then I beg you, . . . send Lazarus to my father's house, for I have five brothers. Let him warn them, so that they will not also come to this place of torment." Abraham replied, "They have Moses and the Prophets; let them listen to them." "No, father Abraham," he said, "but if someone from the dead goes to them, they will repent." He said to him, "If they do not listen to Moses and the Prophets, they will not be convinced even if someone rises from the dead."

—*Luke 16:19–31*

Did you ever use a microscope in seventh grade science class? You peered through the lens, and at the other end you saw amorphous shapes, strange colors—tiny slices of life magnified. The purpose of the microscope is to show us what we cannot see with our naked eye. It magnifies hair, skin cells, bugs, bacteria, grass, pond water—there are no limitations. The microscope has taught us that there is life everywhere.

Dr. E. Stanley Jones, a great missionary in India, told a story about a certain sect of Hindus who wore facemasks over their mouths and noses so that little bugs could not be killed when they breathed. They were shown that the grass upon which they walked also harbored many forms of life that they could not help but step on. When they learned this devastating fact, they solved the problem by destroying the microscope. They did not want to know the truth.

We did the same thing with Jesus. He came into our world and told us the truth: that we are all sinners. So instead of admitting our need for a Savior, we killed Him.

The emphasis in this scripture lesson is the selfish concern for satisfying personal wants and needs. The rich man had everything he could ever need: a beautiful palace, food to eat, luxurious purple robes. Lazarus longed for his scraps to keep him alive, but the rich man wasn't interested. Even the dogs treated Lazarus better, licking his wounds. When they all met in hell, Abraham put the truth under a microscope for the rich man: if his family were not listening to the prophets now, a dead man would not suddenly turn them to godliness. The truth isn't always easy.

Are you living selfishly, like the rich man, or are you living a life that is pleasing to God? If you put your life under a microscope, would you be scared to look?

-50-

The Connection to God

Object:
A cordless telephone

Scripture:

Now Thomas, one of the Twelve, was not with the disciples when Jesus came. So the other disciples told him, "We have seen the Lord!" But he said to them, "Unless I see the nail marks in his hands and put my finger where the nails were, and put my hand into his side, I will not believe it." A week later his disciples were in the house again, and Thomas was with them. Though the doors were locked, Jesus came and stood among them and said, "Peace be with you!" Then He said to Thomas, "Put your finger here; see my hands. Reach out your hand and put it into my side. Stop doubting and believe." Thomas said to Him, "My Lord and my God!" Then Jesus told him, "Because you have seen me, you have believed; blessed are those who have not seen and yet have believed." Jesus did many other miraculous signs in the presence of his disciples, which are not recorded in this book. But these are written that you may believe that Jesus is the Christ, the Son of God, and that by believing you may have life in His name.

—John 20:24–31

Think back to the days when, to make a phone call, you had to lean against the wall, dial your seven digits on the rotary, and stand still for the entire length of your phone call. Luckily, those days are long gone. Eventually, the rotary phones became somewhat mobile: you could drag the phone across the room—maybe twenty feet—but you were still confined by the cord. What a revolution it was when the cordless phone was invented! Now you can take your business anywhere. Start on the couch, maybe you need to go upstairs to print something, then you end up in the kitchen talking while you're cooking dinner.

Now think about how that works. In essence, it's a combination of a telephone and an FM radio transmitter, broadcasting signals over the open airways. With no cord attached, you can send and receive messages through the air, making connections all over the world.

Faith is our connection to God.

One way we demonstrate our faith is through prayer. But your prayer must be genuine. A Pharisee stood in the temple, looked all around, and "prayed with himself." He had no interest in connecting to God, but rather he wanted to hear himself pray. Soon after, the tax collector came in, beat his chest, stood behind a pillar, and prayed to God. "Be merciful to me, a sinner!" Jesus said, "He shall go away justified." When we pray, let us remember that it is God who does the communicating. He tells us to be humble, forgiving, loving, and caring. We don't pray just to hear ourselves talk or feel great about the fact that we're praying. We pray to make a connection with God.

In today's world, we've all witnessed the amazing power of medical technology; cancer therapy and newly discovered vaccines have saved millions of lives. Prayer also has amazing healing powers. Are you hooked up to God?

-51-

Praise the Lord Anyway

Object:
Cork

Scripture:

Be very careful, then, how you live—not as unwise but as wise, making the most of every opportunity, because the days are evil. Therefore do not be foolish, but understand what the Lord's will is. Do not get drunk on wine, which leads to debauchery. Instead, be filled with the Spirit. Speak to one another with psalms, hymns, and spiritual songs. Sing and make music in your heart to the Lord, always giving thanks to God the Father for everything, in the name of our Lord Jesus Christ.

—Ephesians 5:15–20

Cork comes from a tree. It does not dissolve in water, and since it is lightweight and does not absorb water, it floats. For this reason it is used to make lifejackets and fishing bobbers—two things meant to float above water. In the case of a shipwreck or plane crash, that lifejacket can keep a person from drowning, a true lifesaver in case of emergency. Have you ever tried to hold a lifejacket under the water? It's quite impossible! No matter how hard you try, it always comes back up.

Our faith in God is like a cork: It does not soak up the anxieties and sins of the world that can so easily pull us down. It rises above, and it stays above. It cannot be held down. It is our lifejacket when life throws us into a stormy sea.

Let's talk about how we express our faith. Praise and worship is a great place to start. Considering everything that God has done for us, thanking Him is the natural consequence of accepting His will, regardless of what has happened or what will happen. Worship flows naturally from a Spirit-filled person with a thankful heart.

Our lesson from the epistle to the Ephesians touches on this concept. It contrasts the natural practice of man with that of the person praising the Lord under all situations. The practice of man is to vacillate between good and evil. God warns us, however, to walk "not as unwise men" but to be filled with the Spirit. Obviously, we should all make that our goal. But even Christians make mistakes and need love, empathy, and forgiveness. We are imperfect creatures, teaching and preaching imperfectly to an imperfect world. We must recognize our flaws and accept one another.

But facing your humanity isn't always easy. Have you ever thought about the big picture—the whole world? It is full of millions of people, Christian and non-Christian, all of them with their own dreams or lack thereof. Sometimes I look around, and I think, *One hundred years from now, we will all be gone.* That's quite humbling, isn't it?

It's true that one hundred years from now, we will all be gone from this planet. But for those of us who have faith in God, we know that we have the gift of eternity. When we have those moments of fear, resentment, worry, and jealousy, our faith allows us to float back up to the surface and focus on the big picture: our freedom.

-52-

What Is Faith?

Object:
An empty picture frame

Scripture:

Again, the Kingdom of Heaven is like a man who is a merchant seeking fine pearls, who having found one pearl of great price, he went and sold all that he had, and bought it.

—*Matthew 13:45, 46*

Most of you probably have framed pictures all over your houses. Perhaps you have photos of your family at Christmastime, your son's first birthday, a vacation in Mexico, or your daughter's baptism.

But what if the picture disappeared from the frame? An empty frame is kind of sad, isn't it?

Faith puts a picture into the frame of the future. It turns our dreams into reality. It is man's reaction to the plan of God, which we cannot really understand completely. When we feel hopeless and directionless—when the future looks empty— faith fills that hole for us.

God's writer of the book of Hebrews said, "Now faith is

being sure of what we hope for and certain of what we do not see." To someone who is just beginning to grasp the concept of faith, that can be a bit daunting! It's almost like learning to go through the world as a blind person. You have to accept that you don't know what the future holds, but you are confident that God knows what's best for you. When things aren't going your way, you have to respect that it is God's will. Conversely, when life is going smoothly, you should thank Him. With faith, you remember that every moment was planned with a purpose with your future in mind.

So what kind of future does faith bring us? What kind of photo does it place in the frame? The world in the future with faith is a world of peace. It is a brotherhood of man. It is the power of physical healing. It is a world where children will say, "Daddy, what was disease?"

Our scripture tells the story of a pearl merchant who discovers a great treasure and, realizing the value of the pearl, makes it his profession and purpose in life. In fact, he sold all that he had just to buy this one pearl. Why? He knew this was a great investment. Faith is *our* greatest investment. Jesus tells us again and again that faith is the way to Heaven. We need to recognize the value of the treasure He left for us to find.

Jesus said, "Go! It will be done just as you believed it would." Is that really all it takes? By trusting Him, by believing that He knows what's best, we can go forth and accomplish great things. There's no reason to keep an empty picture frame in your home. Fill it with something special.

-53-

The God Dimension

Object:
A Stradivarius violin

Scripture:

Not everyone who says to me, "Lord, Lord," will enter the kingdom of Heaven, but only he who does the will of my Father who is in Heaven
—*Matthew 7:21*

Fritz Kreisler was a world-renowned violinist some years ago. People would travel for miles to see him play his fine Stradivarius violins. To prepare for his highly anticipated concert, one city put up a large billboard with *Stradivarius* in large letters, along with his name. On opening night, the crowds waited eagerly; many of them had purchased their tickets months in advance. The curtain rose. When he started to play, the audience was electrified! They shouted his name in approval. After his first piece, he walked over to the side of the stage, paused while the audience held their breath, and smashed the violin. He stated calmly, "I bought this violin at a secondhand store on the way here for five dollars. Now I shall play on my Stradivarius."

His point? It was not the instrument that mattered, but how the master played it.

We are just like that violin. It doesn't matter how we are built, as long as we let the Lord, our Master, use us.

Today there is an abundance of diverse theological dogma to choose from. We are easily confused by the eloquent and not-so-eloquent voices asking for a following and getting it. There are those who preach hellfire and brimstone as well as those who preach about a loving God who requires no response. Neither of those are true. But we are getting evidence of another dimension, one that the Bible spoke of centuries before Christ. Beyond the God of terror and the God of submission, there is the God who wants us to simply have faith.

Faith is a common theme of the Old Testament. Abraham is a great example of a faithful servant: He left his home in Ur of the Chaldees by faith. He traveled to an unknown land by faith. He met the Lord as a man and was given the promise that his offspring would be like the sands of the sea and the stars of the Heavens. Finally, he was willing to offer his only son, Issac, as an offering to God . . . by faith. Abraham lived in complete obedience to God.

God sent His Son to be the redeemer of the world; we all know that. We receive Christ, He abides in us, and we become children of God. But nowhere in the scriptures does it say that we can sit back and do nothing after that—our salvation is not automatic with baptism. With baptism the relationship is established, but from there on out we must grow into a mature relationship with Christ, accept the gift we have been given, and respond to His love through committed Christian living. We nourish that seed of faith through prayer, Bible study, worship, and service.

John 3:36 tells us, "Whoever believes in the Son has eternal life, but whoever rejects the Son will not see life, for

God's wrath remains on him." So it remains: any of us who are skillfully crafted, but lack faith, will not make beautiful music.

God's Unconditional Love/Forgiveness

-54-

Forgive as God Has Forgiven

Object:
A blackboard and an eraser

Scripture:
"Then Peter came to Jesus and asked, "Lord, how many times shall I forgive my brother when he sins against me? Up to seven times? Jesus answered, "I tell you, not seven times but seventy times seven times."
—*Matthew 18:21–35*

Before PowerPoint presentations, overhead projectors, and even whiteboards, there were blackboards. When you first walk into a classroom, the board is clean—anything can happen. Using chalk you can solve a complicated algebra problem, analyze poetry, or, if you're a student in trouble, write one hundred times what you will not do. If a mistake is made, the teacher can erase it with one swipe of the eraser. But the chalk doesn't disappear on its own; that outside source—the teacher—has to do it.

Luckily for us, God views our sins very much like this.

Although the Bible tells us we are "born in sin," we start off with a clean slate. How do we manage that? Because God sent Jesus to die on the cross for us; in doing so, we are not tied to the dirty slate of Adam and Eve. Jesus said of children, "Of such is the kingdom of God."

David sang this hymn, from Psalm 51:7, a thousand years before Christ: "Wash me and I shall be whiter than snow. . . . Blot out my iniquity." Incredibly, David anticipated the importance of forgiveness.

As you can see from our scripture, Jesus was so committed to this concept that He told Peter the amount of times you should forgive someone is seventy times seven—a countless number. You are to forgive over and over again; no sin is to be remembered. In this same parable, a king was eager to settle accounts with one of his servants. When the servant begged for patience, the king forgave the debt. When that servant went on to demand payment from another servant, however, the king chided and tortured him. "This is how my heavenly father will treat each of you unless you forgive your brother from your heart," he said.

So, like taking an eraser to that calculus problem you just can't get right, we have the luxury of a clean slate. But this doesn't mean we have free reign to act irresponsibly and sinfully. It means that we must turn to God to forgive us and acknowledge that only He has the power to do so.

-55-

A Great Inheritance

Object:
Sand (in a clear bowl)

Scripture:
You are all sons of God through faith in Christ Jesus.
—*Galatians 3:26*

Do you remember being on the beach as a child, building elaborate sand castles—maybe even whole villages? You could use a bucket to make watchtowers, turrets, and a moat. But you had to start somewhere. Sand is everywhere—millions of little grains cover millions of miles of lakeshores, oceans, and beaches. By itself, it is worth very little, but with an architect (or a child with a bucket), it can become something magnificent. It can be the "stuff" of bridges, roads, skyscrapers, and the foundation for millions of homes.

We humans are a lot like sand. There are about 6 billion people on earth; it would seem that we are each small and insignificant. With a little molding from God, however, we can be used for greatness. We all matter.

You have the ability to share the good news. While vacationing in Gatlinburg, Tennessee, Dr. Fred Craddock of Yale Divinity School was enjoying a peaceful dinner out. A distinguished, white-haired man was moving from table to table, and Dr. Craddock really hoped that he would not stop at his table because he didn't want to talk to anyone. But the old man stopped. "Where are you folks from?" he asked. "Oklahoma." "What do you do for a living?" "I teach homiletics at the graduate seminary of Phillips University." "Oh," the old man perked up. "You teach preachers? Have I got a story to tell you!" Dr. Craddock groaned quietly as the man began his story.

"I'm Benn Hooper. I was born not far from here across the mountains. My mother wasn't married when I was born, so I had a hard time. When I started school my classmates called me mean names, so I would go off by myself at recess and during lunch because the taunts hurt me so deeply. What was worse was going downtown every Saturday afternoon and feeling every eye burning a hole through me; they were all wondering who my real father was.

"When I was about twelve years old, a new preacher came to our church. I would always go in late and slip out early. But one day the preacher said the benediction so fast I got caught and had to walk out with the crowd. 'Who are you son? Whose boy are you?' I felt the old weight come on me. Even the preacher was putting me down. But as he looked at my face, he began to smile a big smile of recognition. 'Wait a minute,' he said, 'I know who you are! I see the family resemblance. You are a child of God!' With that he patted me on the shoulder and said, 'Boy, you've got a great inheritance—go claim it!' That was the most important sentence he ever said to me."

This is the potential of every Christian. At times we may feel insignificant, but as children of God, we have a very special birthright. Will you claim yours?

-56-

Forgiven and Restored

Object:
A beat-up twenty dollar bill

Scripture:

So from now on we regard no one from a worldly point of view. Though we once regarded Christ in this way, we do so no longer. Therefore, if anyone is in Christ, he is a new creation; the old has gone, the new has come! All this is from God, who reconciled us to Himself through Christ and gave us the ministry of reconciliation: that God was reconciling the world to Himself in Christ, not counting men's sins against them. And He has committed to us the message of reconciliation. We are therefore Christ's ambassadors, as though God were making His appeal through us. We implore you on Christ's behalf: Be reconciled to God. God made Him who had no sin to be sin for us, so that in Him we might become the righteousness of God.

—*2 Corinthians 5:16–21*

Have you ever seen one of those twenty-dollar bills with a stamp on it directing you to a Web site where you can trace the bill? It's an interesting concept: you can follow a single bill from Dallas to Albuquerque to Little Rock to Asheville.

It will change hands so many times, get folded into many wallets—scruffy ones and nice, expensive ones—and probably get stuffed into many pockets. Eventually, it will just be a soft, sliver of a thing, and someone will deem it unfit for circulation.

But up until that last moment, it always had the same value as it did when it was a crisp, new bill. If I hand the cashier my dirty twenty-dollar bill, he has to take it. It will buy me the same amount of groceries as a new bill.

As Christians, we are here to see the dignity of every human, to view every human as a potential child of God. Some of us have been put through the wringer. Some of us are downtrodden, some of us are poised, some of us are frail, some of us are strong. It is not our responsibility to determine who is of greater value. That is why God sent His Son into a very rebellious world—to redeem it for Himself and for eternal glory.

Our Gospel demonstrates God's redeeming power. We are not to look at people through a worldly lens—one that judges, criminalizes, and compares—but rather we should view everyone the way God does—in a loving and forgiving manner. How can you go about judging others, when God has given you the ultimate gift of redemption for your defects? Paul tells the Corinthians plainly, "Christ does not count your sins against you." God's hope in sending his Son to redeem us was that we might too become righteous.

You can work on forgiveness one step at a time. If a friend hurts your feelings—perhaps at the last minute he calls off a dinner you'd planned—remember all of the other times this friend has been there for you. Focus on the good, not the bad. Your twenty-dollar bill might be rumpled, but at least you've got twenty dollars.

-57-

Shaped to Perfection

Object:
A diamond

Scripture:

A voice of one calling in the desert, "Prepare the way for the Lord, make straight paths for him. Every valley shall be filled in, every mountain and hill made low. The crooked roads shall become straight, the rough ways smooth. And all mankind will see God's salvation."

—*Luke 3:3–6*

Whenever you watch heist movies, what is it the black-masked thieves are always after? Diamonds! That's because diamonds are one of the most prized objects in the world.

Diamonds have been prized and sought after for years, ever since man observed the crystallization of carbon. But in the beginning, diamonds are the same as coal: cheap, black, and full of impurities. Can you imagine tossing diamonds onto your grill or into your fireplace? Of course not. With a little time and pressure, however, the substances hardens and purifies, and it becomes something beautiful and precious. The more pure and clear, the more valuable it is.

Eventually, it is cut down into many facets so that it will reflect light.

We are born into the blackness of sin. By the grace of God, we are purified. We are pressed, hardened, and cut to conform to what our Maker wants. As we are cut down, we lose a part of ourselves, but we begin to reflect God. Then we are free from death, and we become children of God. The light of eternity shines through us. "Let your light so shine before men!" He tells us.

One of the great problems of religion is that when God wants us for His own, He prunes and trims us to His dimensions. We are men, however, so we still falter and desire to go our own way. We want the comfort of religion without the sacrifice and peace without participation.

But the way of man is not what leads to eternity. The way of man leads to hate, crime, coveting, violence, idolatry, gossip, lying, adultery, and selfishness. The way of man has led to millennia of warfare. The way of man has outlawed prayer. The way of man is not pleasing to God.

It's time to turn back in God's direction. Jesus said, "For I tell you that unless your righteousness surpasses that of the Pharisees and the teachers of the law, you will certainly not enter the kingdom of heaven." That's a stern warning! He makes it clear that we must live our lives according to God's plan for us if we want eternal life. So which are you: a piece of black coal, or a sparkling diamond?

-58-

Preparations

Object:
A pad of paper and a pencil

Scripture:

As John's disciples were leaving, Jesus began to speak to the crowd about John: "What did you go out into the desert to see? A reed swayed by the wind? If not, what did you go out to see? A man dressed in fine clothes? No, those who wear fine clothes are in kings' palaces. Then what did you go out to see? A prophet? Yes, I tell you, and more than a prophet. This is the one about whom it is written: "I will send my messenger ahead of you, who will prepare your way before you.""

—Matthew 11:7–10

What is the very first thing you remember learning in school? Before algebra and poetry and the state capitals, you learned your ABCs. Now think of everything you know today that you can do because you know the alphabet: you can write your name in cursive, you can write text messages to your friends, and you can write an essay comparing *Hamlet* and *King Lear*. It all started with that basic preparation: your teacher holding up colorful cards with letters on them.

Everything we do requires some kind of preparation. We learn the numbers before we can do complicated calculus. We must crawl before we can walk. We have to warm up before we can run a marathon. We pay our dues at the bottom of the ladder before we can run the company.

We must also make preparations as Christians. We all begin with a loose idea of God: beautiful and loving, or terrible and judging, depending on your perspective. This reminds me of a story about a little boy who was drawing a picture during Sunday school. "What are you drawing?" his friend asked. "A picture of God." "Well, that is good, but how can you draw a picture of God when no one know what He looks like?" "Well," he said, "they will when I finish this picture!"

At some point, we take faltering baby steps into our faith. Through prayer, service, fellowship, and church attendance, we grow. As we learn more, we are able to live Christian lives of sacrifice.

God made preparations for His great sacrifice, in which he sent His Son to die for us. God had given the first rights of evangelism to the Jews, but in the centuries of relative quiet before Jesus's birth, the preparation was mere expectation: every family thought that perhaps the prophet would be their first-born son. So God sent John the Baptist to prepare the people for the coming of Jesus. Luke writes: "And you, my child, will be called a prophet of the Most High; for you will go on before the Lord to prepare the way for Him, to give His people the knowledge of salvation through the forgiveness of their sins, because of the tender mercy of our God . . . from heaven to shine on those living in darkness and in the shadow of death, to guide our feet into the path of peace." By sending John ahead to lead the way, the people were all the more ready to hear Jesus's message of hope.

The world's most inspirational leaders didn't get to where they are now by relying on luck. They brainstormed, put in overtime, and fought for what they wanted. The world's greatest engineering marvels—the Bird's Nest Stadium, Lake Mead, the Channel Tunnel—all began with a pen and paper. What preparations have you made?

-59-

The Power of Weakness

Object:
A pearl

Scripture:

To keep me from becoming conceited because of these surpassingly great revelations, there was given me a thorn in my flesh, a messenger of Satan, to torment me. Three times I pleaded with the Lord to take it away from me. But he said to me, "My grace is sufficient for you, for my power is made perfect in weakness." Therefore I will boast all the more gladly about my weaknesses, so that Christ's power may rest on me.

—2 Corinthians 12:7–9

Have you ever worn beautiful pearl jewelry? Pearls have been highly valued objects of beauty for thousands of years. But did you know that the pearl inside the oyster is actually the result of irritation? Down on the seafloor, the oyster is somehow opened and a tiny grain of sand slips in. The grain has sharp edges, and it irritates the soft, delicate oyster. So the oyster covers the sand with coats of calcium (like trying to get rid of an annoying itch). The result is a shiny, smooth, mother of pearl.

Just like the little grain of sand, God often leaves us "thorns in the flesh." He purposely leaves us with a weakness, so that we must fight—looking to Him—to overcome it. The weakness is covered by layers of spiritual growth, and the result is that we are smoother and stronger because of it, like a pearl of spiritual understanding and divine direction.

Paul, like many men, was tested by God. The book of Acts tells us the story of his conversion: Having received divine direction, he began his ministry when blinded on the road to Damascus on his way to persecute Christians. "Lord, what would you have me do?" he cried. He saw the hand of God in the remaking of himself. Paul understood the greatness of God, and it was then that he found communion with God. He was content, knowing that his bodily suffering was incidental compared to the eternal glory that would be his.

So what do we take from this? When cutting, painful events occur in our lives—from a goldfish dying to going through a divorce to having a loved one with cancer—God wants us to cover these things with love and prayer. Every time we pray or turn to our loved ones in our time of need, we add a new thickness layer, like the oyster that covers the grain of sand with layer after layer of calcium. With Jesus's love emanating from inside of us, we will eventually come out smooth and pearly.

-60-

Spiritual vs. Physical Health

Object:
Pills

Scripture:

Praise the Lord, O my soul; all my inmost being, praise His holy name. Praise the Lord, O my soul, and forget not all His benefits—who forgives all your sins and heals all your diseases, who redeems your life from the pit and crowns you with love and compassion, who satisfies your desires with good things so that your youth is renewed like the eagle's.

—Psalm 103:1–5

Think of the last time you were watching TV. How many different commercials did you see for different medication? Lipozolve promises to "dissolve your fat." Follicleanse claims it will "stimulate circulation for faster hair growth." Anoretix alleges it can help you lose twelve pounds in two weeks by suppressing your appetite. And what about those drugs that aren't advertised, but that doctors freely hand out prescriptions for? Addictive pain pills, sedatives, and amphetamines are thought to be a quick fix for all of our problems. Could there be another solution?

When you read the Bible and really comprehend it, it comes to life; when you are truly engaged, it can affect your body, mind, and soul. The Bible helps a person to know who he or she is, and it also teaches that there is a loving and caring God. How does God's Word nurture us to health? It teaches us to forgive others as God forgives us. Numerous studies have proven the detrimental effects of stress on the body, so in letting go of resentment we are improving our health. God's Word tells us to love our neighbor as ourselves. Doing good things for others will make you feel better about yourself.

For millennia, man survived without the kinds of medication we rely on today. What if Jesus's followers had told Him, "It's OK, Teacher, we don't need you to heal this leper. We have a pill that will help him," or "No worries, Jesus, I'd rather you not wash my feet today. I can just spray a cleansing tonic on them." Jesus might have been offended (of course, He wouldn't hold this against anyone).

With the advances in scientific technology, we've come to believe that medication is always the solution. Are you easily distracted? Pop a pill. Feeling a little anxious? Take this little white one. Wish you had more hair, stronger fingernails, smoother skin? Done, done, and done.

Medication can surely solve some of your physical ailments. But what about your spiritual ailments—the God dimension? Maybe you have a great job, a loving family, and good health, but there's still something missing and you just can't put your finger on it. Write a prescription for God. The doctor's instructions? Read your Bible. Go to church. Pray. You'd be amazed how much more alive you'll feel.

-61-

Sealed for Sending!

Object:
A ceramic vase

Scripture:

And do not grieve the Holy Spirit of God, with whom you were sealed for the day of redemption. Get rid of all bitterness, rage and anger, brawling and slander, along with every form of malice. Be kind and compassionate to one another, forgiving each other, just as in Christ God forgave you.
—Ephesians 4:30–32

Have you ever watched a potter at work? She works very purposefully and deliberately, such that each and every turn of her pinky has meaning. Vases have been a prized object of beauty for thousands of years, because each one is crafted individually, shaped, fired, and painted for uniqueness. They come from all over the world—Mexico, Australia, South Africa—and you see them in almost every home.

Some vases are expensive and elaborate. Others are plain and simple. All of them, however, serve a purpose. Perhaps you have a vase that contains an ever-changing assortment of lilies, tulips, and gardenias. Maybe you have two vases, and you use them as bookends. Or, perhaps your priceless vase from Morocco is simply for decoration and nostalgia.

We are like vases. No matter what we look like—fancy or plain—God has crafted us for a purpose. If the hairs of our head are numbered, as the Bible states, and God knows when a sparrow falls to the ground, then God has a purpose for each of us. The Bible speaks of how God is the Creator (the potter) and we are the clay. He will use each and every one of us, if we let Him.

God calls us—His children. He calls us the same way He called Paul: "Paul, an apostle—sent not from men nor by man, but by Jesus Christ and God the Father, who raised him from the dead." Like Paul, we are sealed up, bound for the purpose of God by the Holy Spirit. Before we can be molded, however, we must have knowledge of what we really are. That knowledge requires awareness of and sorrow for our sin, which is in contrast to God. When we learn that we are so different from Him, we are eager to be shaped. According to Ephesians, "In your anger do not sin: Do not let the sun go down while you are still angry." That is, no matter how difficult it is to face yourself, use this realization to reshape yourself in God's likeness.

We all remember playing with clay in art class. Do you remember what happened when you left it sitting out too long? It dried up! Are you letting God mold you?

-62-

One Dark Spot

Object:
A white canvas with a dark spot on it

Scripture:

Repent therefore and be converted, that your sins may be blotted out, so that times of refreshing may come from the presence of the Lord.

—*Acts 3:19*

Imagine a large, blank canvas. With an artist and a brush, this could become a beautiful impressionist piece, or a flowing Tuscan landscape, or a fascinating modernist creation.

Now imagine that same canvas with a big black paint splotch on it. No longer are you thinking about the potential of that canvas. All you see is that black spot.

Sin is like that. Very often when someone we know has sinned, that is all we can see. We forget about all the years Susan put into directing the church choir. We forget that Gayle has been volunteering at the homeless shelter every Saturday for twenty years. We forget about all the blood, sweat, and tears Daniel put into organizing the canned food drive. We no longer see the good, or the years of sacrifice, caring, and love. All we see is that sin.

Did you know, however, that this is the very reason that God sent His Son to Earth? He made this great sacrifice to remove the dark spot of sin from humanity. 1 John reminds us that all we need to do is humble ourselves and confess our wrongdoings: "If we confess our sins, He is faithful and just and will forgive us our sins and purify us from all unrighteousness." God loves us so much that He will forgive all our sins, big and small.

A good mentor can make a huge difference when it comes to cleaning up our lives. Many studies of hardened criminals tell us that the big reason that these men are in prison is not because of poverty, lack of education, or any other common assumption. The big reason, according to the men themselves, is that they did not have a mentor—a coach, a pastor, or teacher—to help them set goals for themselves.

Sounds simple, right?

Even grown men can benefit from the positive influence of a good leader. Many years ago, "Hollywood" Henderson was a star linebacker for the Dallas Cowboys, but he had a lot of personal demons. Eventually, Coach Landry had enough of his flamboyant lifestyle, and he let him go. But that didn't stop him. Hollywood's destructive routine of drugs, alcohol, and women did not stop until he was thrown into jail. It was in rehab where he finally cleaned up his life for good. Today, he is a model of propriety and travels around the country speaking to kids about the pitfalls of drugs. Even though it took awhile, one single person changed his life.

Commitment to Jesus as Lord and Savior has saved millions of other lives as well. Because only Jesus, as God, can forgive sin. No matter how dirty your canvas, turning to Jesus will give you a bright new future.

-63-

Where Do We Go from Here?

Object:
A pumpkin

Scripture:

The Lord said . . . "I will sprinkle you with clean water, and you will be clean. . . . I will take away your stubborn heart and give you a new heart. . . . You will have only pure thoughts, because I will put my Spirit in you."

—*Ezekiel 36:16, 25–28*

A woman had recently been baptized, and one of her co-workers asked her what it was like to be a Christian. Caught off guard, she wasn't quite sure how to answer. When she noticed a jack-o-lantern on her desk, however, she knew.

"It's like being a pumpkin."

The co-worker was stumped and asked her to explain.

"Well," she said, "God picks you from the patch and brings you in and washes off all the dirt that you got from being around all the other pumpkins. Then He cuts off the top and takes out all that yucky stuff from the inside. He removes all those seeds of doubt, hate, greed, etc. Then He carves you a new smiling face and puts His light inside of you so people can see you shining from far away. It is our choice to either stay outside and rot on the vine or let God carve us into something unique."

God wants to make us over; He has a plan for our lives, and He would hate to see that go to waste. He wants the light of Christ to shine from within us, so that all the world can see us.

Let's talk a little bit about change. We'll start with some history: We were created in the image of God, but we rebelled. So God sent Moses to Mt. Sinai to deliver the Ten Commandments, giving us new guidelines on how to live in harmony with God. We extended those commandments into hundreds of nitpicking laws and rules, to the point that we lost heart. So God sent His Son to forgive mankind their sins, and Jesus sent the Holy Spirit to give us new birth.

So the basis for change lies within each of us: we have free will ("for all men have sinned and fall short of the glory of God"). We have to make the choice to come to God and allow Him to change us. When we come to God—warts and all—we give ourselves over through faith, which connects us to what is eternal and everlasting.

You hear from a lot of climbers that they love to climb mountains, but they hate going uphill. They say, "Trails need to be reconstructed. Please avoid building trails that go uphill. Please build more chairlifts so we don't have to hike." Well, what's the point? Why go into something if you're not giving one hundred percent? In the same way, when we give ourselves over to God, we go with full faith, knowing that He will mold us to His will, with His good intentions. Why hold on to all that yucky stuff inside, when the Artist can mold you into something beautiful?

-64-

Love Covers

Object:
A blanket

Scripture:

Dear friends, do not be surprised at the painful trial you are suffering, as though something strange were happening to you. But rejoice that you participate in the sufferings of Christ, so that you may be overjoyed when His glory is revealed. If you are insulted because of the name of Christ, you are blessed, for the Spirit of glory and of God rests on you.

—1 Peter 4:12–14

Did you have security blanket when you were a child? One you took with you everywhere you went? Perhaps you were even reluctant to give it up as an adult?

Blankets serve a pretty basic purpose: they cover us, protect us, and keep us warm in the cold. You see tiny babies covered up, regardless of the weather.

As growing Christians we are tender, and like little children, we need a blanket. God provides that for us. He sees our sinful nature, but he covers it. He protects us from the dangerous elements of the world around us. In fact, when He sent His Son to die for us, we were protected from that time on.

Many years ago I heard a story about a group of American soldiers at the front lines in Korea. An enemy soldier lobbed a hand grenade directly at them. One brave soldier immediately threw his body over the grenade and it exploded, killing him but saving the others. Because of his act of sacrifice, all the other soldiers lived. John 15:13 says, "Greater love has no one than this, that he lay down his life for his friends."

Let's take a look at our scripture. 1 Peter is a pretty remarkable book, which covers a lot of different ideas, but the chief point throughout is that, when persecution comes, we must stand firm in Christ. Keep in mind, back when this was written, early Christians were being horribly persecuted by Rome. They wanted merely to live their lives just as we do today. So the people who received this letter had the same problems we do: the flesh versus the Spirit, the will of God versus the will of man.

The flesh is all about satisfying human needs and desires without regard for God or others. It is human passion: licentiousness, lust, drunkenness, idolatry. It may feel great now, but God will judge us after death ("But they will have to give account to Him who is ready to judge the living and the dead"). The Spirit is all about kindness, goodness, gentleness, and self-control; it focuses on ways that we can glorify God and love our neighbor.

It's not always easy to make the right decision—to side with the will of God. This letter from 1 Peter, however, describes the rewards of doing so. We may be persecuted for our beliefs. Even though blatant discrimination and public harassment (the kind the early Christians faced) is illegal today, many of us may have been bullied or prodded because of what we believe. The good news is that "the Spirit of glory and of God" rests on us. Whatever we face now will be long forgotten in the long scheme of eternity. God's love covers us; we have a way to stay warm as the world gets colder and colder.

Love thy Neighbor

-65-

A Good Seed

Object:
Two apples, one good and one wormy

Scripture:

On one occasion an expert in the law stood up to test Jesus. "Teacher," he asked, "what must I do to inherit eternal life?" "What is written in the Law?" He replied. "How do you read it?" He answered: "'Love the Lord your God with all your heart and with all your soul and with all your strength and with all your mind'; and, 'Love your neighbor as yourself.'" "You have answered correctly," Jesus replied. "Do this and you will live." But he wanted to justify himself, so he asked Jesus, "And who is my neighbor?" In reply Jesus said: "A man was going down from Jerusalem to Jericho, when he fell into the hands of robbers. They stripped him of his clothes, beat him and went away, leaving him half dead. A priest happened to be going down the same road, and when he saw the man, he passed by on the other side. So too, a Levite, when he came to the place and saw him, passed by on the other side. But a Samaritan, as he traveled, came where the man was; and when he saw him, he took pity on him. He went to him and bandaged his wounds, pouring on oil and wine. Then he put the man on his own donkey, took him to an inn and took care of him. The next day he took out two silver coins and gave them to the innkeeper. 'Look after him,' he said, 'and when I return, I will reimburse you for any extra expense you may have.' Which of these three do you think was a neighbor to the man who fell into the hands of robbers?" The expert in the law replied, "The one who had mercy on him." Jesus told him, "Go and do likewise."

—Luke 10:25–37

Imagine you've got two apples on a table. One is round, red, and shiny. The other is shriveled, brown, and rotten; it probably smells. Which would you like to eat? Which would you give to a teacher? The answer is easy.

Such a small amount of care would have made the wormy apple good and healthy. If you're thinking that worms crawled into a perfectly healthy apple and destroyed it, think again. Little worm eggs get into the apple at the earliest stage—when the apples are still in the bud; later the eggs hatch and the worms grow inside the apples. So, it takes a lot of care and treatment early on to keep the apples healthy.

So it is with us: we can get some pretty rotten ideas in our hearts and minds as little children, and those bad seeds will keep growing if we're not properly cared for. If seven-year-old Tim plays a violent video game, for example, eggs of sin will be planted if his mother does not tell him afterward that it's not moral and normal to kill people. When little Tim becomes a teenager, he may take a gun to school because he learned that guns make him a winner. As an adult, he might beat his wife because his video game taught him that women are dispensable. All it would have taken to stop those seeds from becoming worms was a little nurturing.

The good Samaritan story demonstrates a lack of concern for human need. Two highly esteemed men, a priest and a Levite, ignored a man in need. All it took was a little bit of neighborly concern from one Samaritan, however, to teach the lesson. God expects every one of us to be nurturing. It is so important, in fact, that He commands it second only to loving Him!

So think about the last time you were kind to a stranger. Are you a good apple?

-66-

One Body

A bouquet of flowers with a card that says "I love you"

The blind receive sight, the lame walk, those who have leprosy are cured, the deaf hear, the dead are raised, and the good news is preached to the poor. Blessed is the man who does not fall away on account of me.
—*Matthew 11:5–6*

Imagine you're standing at the baggage claim at an airport. One by one, people exit the plane and stream down the hall: a man in a business suit, a young woman and her daughter, an elderly couple, a family of four, a teenager traveling alone. As all of these people turn the corner, they greet waiting family and friends, and the room is suddenly filled with smiling faces: people laughing and telling stories and saying "I love you."

When someone plays the right chords on a piano, you get tonal harmony. If someone hands you a bouquet of beautiful flowers, you get visual harmony. When someone says "I love you," you've got harmony among men.

This is God's purpose for us. The Word of God reveals this to us again and again (and you see it demonstrated at weddings, anniversaries, and funerals day after day): even if life is taken away, love is eternal.

Harmony in its most basic sense often refers to music: it is a synchronizing of tonal vibrations that produces a pleasant sound sensation. That song you just can't get enough of? Most likely, a musician put in a lot of effort perfecting the dissonance—that moment where you cringe—so that it slips into a resolution. When each chord is matched just so, you get harmony.

In another sense, harmony is anything that is pleasing to God. It is the uplifting quality of bringing out the image of God, in man, in the body of Christ. We are many different people making up one body; when we love each other fully and work together deliberately, it creates a beautiful harmony. When we feel dissonance, it is merely man pushing for resolution with God.

When that happens, what can you do to create harmony? Start by introducing yourself to your neighbor. A single kind word can go a long way. When you get home, pray for that person. It doesn't have to be long; perhaps just thank God, and pray for this person's health. The next step is a bit harder. Think about the person who has done you the greatest harm. Pray for this person. Does this sound difficult? It's supposed to be. This is one step toward eliminating resentment, however— something that causes dissonance rather than harmony. Now you can pray that God forgives you for harboring that resentment. You already know God forgives you. Now move on.

How do you feel?

-67-

Slow Down

Object:
A trumpet

Scripture:

A new command I give you: Love one another. As I have loved you, so you must love one another.

—*John 13:34*

If someone walked up behind you and blew into a trumpet right now, how would you react? You'd probably be angry, because someone blew a loud horn in your ear. You'd tell that person it's not necessary to be that close to get your attention. You can hear a trumpet from far away; it makes a beautiful, brassy sound.

A young executive had recently gotten a shiny, new Jaguar convertible. He had the top down, sunglasses on, and music blaring; he was very proud to be speeding down the road in his new wheels. Suddenly, he heard a big *thump*—someone had thrown a brick against the door of his car! He jumped out and ran over to a little boy standing nearby. He tried to keep his composure as the frightened little boy held back tears. "I didn't know what else to do!" he cried. "It's my brother—he rolled off the curb and fell out of his wheelchair, and I can't lift him up." He was sobbing at this point. "Would you please help me get him back in his wheelchair? He's hurt and he's too heavy for me." After a cursory glance at the dent in his door, the young man gently lifted the boy back into his wheelchair. Then he took his clean handkerchief and wiped away the scrapes and cuts. The little boy said, "Thank you, and God bless you!"

The young man never did get his door fixed. He kept it as a reminder not to go through life so fast that someone has to throw a brick to get your attention.

It's important to God that we take the time to look around, listen, and help others. What if God stopped loving and caring for us because we weren't returning the favor?

Our scripture comes from John 13. The disciples were shocked that their teacher, Jesus, was washing their feet. But Jesus was trying to set an example. "Now that I, your Lord and Teacher, have washed your feet," He told them, "you also should wash one another's feet. I have set you an example that you should do as I have done for you." It was important to Jesus that they learn to love one another as He loved them.

Has anyone ever had to go to extremes to get your attention? Do you ever get so distracted, caught up in mundane details of life that you don't notice the truly important things? Just for one day, consider moving a bit slower and listening a bit more. See if you feel any different.

-68-

The Seasons of Growth

Object:
Mother

Scripture:

If you love me, you will obey what I command. And I will ask the Father, and He will give you another Counselor to be with you forever— the Spirit of truth. . . . But you know Him, for He lives with you and will be in you. I will not leave you as orphans; I will come to you. Before long, the world will not see me anymore, but you will see me. Because I live, you also will live. On that day you will realize that I am in my Father, and you are in me, and I am in you. . . . He who loves me will be loved by my Father, and I too will love him and show myself to him.

—John 14:15–21

A kindergartner named Eddie was acting out every day in school, and even though the teacher continually sent him to the principal's office, he wasn't improving. One day, he stole a crayon from another student and lied about it. The teacher had learned that previous discipline was futile, so she said, "I guess I'll have to call your mother and tell her what you've been up to." Eddie started to cry: "Please don't tell my mother!

She thinks I'm a good boy, and she would be very sad! I'll behave from now on, I promise!"

As we can see from Eddie's story, mothers have a very important role in our development and growth. Abraham Lincoln himself said, "All that I am or hope to be I owe to my angel mother." What a lot of people don't know is that he was referring to his stepmother, who raised him after the death of his mother. "Mother" can mean many things to different people.

We all know that babies need a mother right away. A baby cannot feed itself or change its own clothes or diapers. During this time of dependence, a baby learns to crawl, then walk, then run, and eventually it learns to communicate. Personality develops, depending on the encouragement and/or discipline the parents give. In the middle stage of development, children begin to test the waters, learning from their mistakes. In the final stage of development, they learn to love. They love their parents, but they are independent enough to survive without them.

Jesus's followers went through all of these stages of development, as demonstrated in our scripture. In the beginning, God became flesh in order to give His words relevance. Jesus was there to personally deliver God's message, perform miracles, and act as a teacher to the Apostles. Christ, along with his Apostles, led His people slowly. Paul told the Corinthians: "I gave you milk, not solid food, for you were not yet ready for it." If Christ had walked on water before first teaching His people anything about God, they might have been afraid. Eventually, however, they were ready. He told them, "Before long, the world will not see me anymore." He knew He would be crucified, but He assured them that He would come back and that He and God were one.

What stage of spiritual development are you in? For those of us who are spiritually children, we can't have Jesus here to physically hold our hand or feed us bread. We do, however, have friends and members of the congregation to guide us to maturity. Others of us have already "cut the cord"; if that's you, could you be doing more to nurture other members of your congregation?

-69-

It Only Takes a Spark

Object:
A spark plug

Scripture:

Moses describes in this way the righteousness that is by the law: "The man who does these things will live by them." But the righteousness that is by faith says: "Do not say in your heart, 'Who will ascend into heaven?'" (that is, to bring Christ down) "or 'Who will descend into the deep?'" (that is, to bring Christ up from the dead). But what does it say? "The word is near you; it is in your mouth and in your heart," that is, the word of faith we are proclaiming: That if you confess with your mouth, "Jesus is Lord," and believe in your heart that God raised him from the dead, you will be saved. For it is with your heart that you believe and are justified, and it is with your mouth that you confess and are saved.

—Romans 10:5–10

Even if you've never actually seen one, I have a feeling most of you know what a spark plug is. It's the thing that makes an engine run, when all the other parts—the cylinder, the valves, the piston—are in order. Even a perfect engine, without a spark plug, will not run.

A spark plug must be in place in the engine to be effective. You could buy the most expensive, high-value spark plug there is, but if it's collecting dust on a shelf somewhere, it's worthless. A lot of church members are up on the shelf: they don't ever get connected to the moving parts, to the power of God.

Once it's in the car, that spark plug needs to actually be connected to the battery and the engine. So it is with us, to bear fruit as Christians, we need to be connected to the battery (God) and with the engine (people).

Many years ago I heard a story about a woman named Beverly Moss. She had stopped by the local pool on her way home from work, so she was wearing a tailored suit and high heels. She was chatting with some friends when she noticed a three-year-old girl, Natalie, floundering in the deep end. The little girl's mother was too terrified to scream. Two young men sunbathing nearby saw the little girl struggling, but they did not move either. Beverly didn't think twice; she dived into the water, all the way into the bottom where the girl had sunk all the way down. She swam to the top, laboring with the girl in her arms, where she resuscitated her. Beverly thought nothing of this—she was saving a little girl's life. Sparked by her love for others, she had no concern for her fancy suit or her hair. It was spontaneous, the way a spark plug sparks a fire so the engine will move.

God wants us to be little spark plugs. He wants us to dive right in, lighting fires and spreading the good news that He loves us and that we are saved.

You've heard it said, "It only takes a spark to get a fire going." Perhaps that little girl that Beverly saved will grow up forever grateful to the stranger who saved her life, in turn bestowing kind words and blessings upon everyone she meets. Every prayer, every kind word, every good deed is a spark that can start a fire. If you're on the shelf, get connected. See if you can light a fire everywhere you go.

-70-

What Am I Living For?

Object:
The straws of a broom

Scripture:

Dear friends, let us love one another, for love comes from God. Everyone who loves has been born of God and knows God. Whoever does not love does not know God, because God is love. This is how God showed his love among us: He sent His one and only Son into the world that we might live through Him. This is love: not that we loved God, but that He loved us and sent His Son as an atoning sacrifice for our sins. Dear friends, since God so loved us, we also ought to love one another. No one has ever seen God; but if we love one another, God lives in us and His love is made complete in us.

—1 John 4:7–12

Imagine trying to sweep your floor with broom that only has one straw on it. That would be a painstakingly difficult task! You could take that single straw and snap it in half easily. So that one straw by itself is worthless, but if you take hundreds of straws and tie them together, you've got a tool that can clean an entire house.

We Christians are a lot like that broom. One person can't always do much. One person can't always withstand the temptations around him or her and might break just like the single straw. But when we are bound together in love, like the string that binds the straws in the broom, we can do a lot. United in Christ, the handle that guides us and powers us, we can help clean up the world and sweep the evil out of our homes, cities, and nations!

Have you ever asked yourself what you're living for?

A reporter came to a building site and asked three different men what they were doing.

One said, "I'm working eight hours a day laying bricks."

Another said, "I'm making seventy dollars a day laying bricks!"

The third said, "I'm building a cathedral!"

A couple of weeks later the reporter returned to find the third man missing. "What happened?" he asked.

"Well, he was fired. We are not building a cathedral; we're building a gas station."

These three men all had different goals; they weren't working together. Having goals, however, can make all the difference. A World War II soldier was sick but didn't tell anyone because he wanted to go to college on the Army Specialized Training Program. Close to death, he had a vision of Jesus, who came to him asking, "Have you told anyone about me?" That invigorated him, and he was inspired to finish medical school and start the Christian Youth Corps.

It's hard to avoid seeing all the evil in the world. 9/11 heralded a new era of fear for all of us. Ill-intentioned people have assumed leadership roles all over the world—North Korea, Afghanistan, Iran, Zimbabwe. Sometimes we feel powerless to stop it. We can't do it alone, but if we work together in God's name, we can take small steps toward making the world a better place for all of us.

-71-

Fellowship

Object:
A cookie cutter

Scripture:

This is the message we have heard from him and declare to you: God is light; in Him there is no darkness at all. If we claim to have fellowship with Him yet walk in the darkness, we lie and do not live by the truth. But if we walk in the light, as He is in the light, we have fellowship with one another, and the blood of Jesus, His Son, purifies us from all sin.

—1 John 1:7–7

A really great tradition for a lot of people at Christmas is making cookies. Mix the dough, roll the dough, shape the dough, bake the dough. You can make all kinds of shapes: Christmas trees, bells, snowmen, stars, and candy canes. Or maybe you want all snowmen? Easy. You've got a cookie cutter.

Today you can get cookie cutters that come in all sorts of strange shapes: Baking cookies for your daughter's graduation? Try the mortarboards. Your toddler's birthday? Flamingos and stegosauruses. Throwing a party at your beach house? Put together an assortment of iced mermaids, surfboards, and palm trees. There is no limit to the identical shapes you can make.

We humans, on the other hand, are nothing like cookie cutters. You've heard that no one alive has a fingerprint like yours. Even twins are different. In the Bible God said, "Let us create man in our image." You could deduce from that statement, then, that we are all alike. But we're not. God created each of us with a specific plan in mind. We are all God's children, all unique, all made to love one another.

This epistle, 1 John, is an important one that discusses fellowship. It says that if we "walk in the light, as He is in the light," then we will be in fellowship with one another. Unfortunately, there are plenty of people in this world who do not love their neighbor. There are bitter people out there—people scarred by tragedy, people disheartened by failure, and people led by false Gods or no God—who want to bring others down. But that shouldn't stop us. The good news is that others all over the world have experienced the love of Jesus Christ, and the movement is unstoppable.

This epistle also tells us we have to walk the walk: "If we claim to be without sin, we deceive ourselves and the truth is not in us." For us, there is no claiming to be without sin, because we are all imperfect people. But Jesus said, "The entire law is summed up in a single command: 'Love your neighbor as yourself.'" Think that's always easy? I am imperfect, and my neighbor is imperfect, and we are all brothers in Christ, so we are to love each other.

When God created us, He didn't use a cookie cutter. He didn't need any special tool, because He is perfect. He used His bare hands, rolling and pinching and shaping us to His liking. Thus we are each unique, with tiny details that make us special. Don't begrudge your neighbor his imperfections. Let's be in fellowship with one another instead, celebrating the things that make us different.

-72-

Where It All Began
(Pentecost sermon)

Object:
A brick

Scripture:

And everyone who calls on the name of the Lord will be saved.

—*Acts 2:21*

Have you ever looked down and seen a single brick on the ground in front of you? Probably not. Bricks are one of those things that come in units. A bricklayer starts by laying one brick on the ground, but he immediately surrounds it with others. This is because bricks are used for a purpose: they are not meant to look nice (in fact, they're not the most aesthetically pleasing), but rather they are meant to build strong structures.

People were designed for a purpose as well: to build God's kingdom.

One brick can do very little by itself. But many bricks, held together by mortar, form the most beautiful mansions, walls, gardens, and roadways. So it is with us, a single person cannot do very much, but when we all stick together, according to God's plan, we can build His kingdom.

We were taught to pray, "Thy kingdom come, thy will be done." But how and when did this all begin?

Pentecost is the feast of the harvest, and it takes place fifty days after Passover. At the time, the world was in crisis: Rome was in power, taxes were high, revolution was in the air, and false messiahs abounded. The Jews suffered from political faction, and slavery was widespread. The Jews, the chosen people, had gathered in Rome to tell people about the Christ. Jesus had promised that, about fifty days after the resurrection, the Holy Spirit would come, The Bible tells us the disciples were in the Upper Room waiting as Jesus had told them to. As He promised, the Holy Spirit returned. Jesus said, "Peace be with you! As the Father has sent me, I am sending you." That moment in A.D. 29 in Jerusalem was the foundation of the Christian Church.

On that day, the people heard the message, and they heard it in their own language. The disciples were filled with the fire of the Holy Spirit. So what was the message?

The whole purpose of Pentecost was to evangelize to the entire world. They told of the mighty works of God through the Christ. They spoke for God (prophecy). They became the fulfillment for Christ's promise. They were the spark that lit the flame, all starting in that small room in Jerusalem. Literally, the Church began in that room, but really it started with the heart of God; it will continue to touch the world through the Holy Spirit.

J. Edgar Hoover said, "Let us work for a revolution, a revolution by the Spirit, not by the sword!" If only everyone listened to him! Hoover saw the benefit of working together. We are each but one small piece—one little brick—in God's house. If you remove one, there is a giant hole. We need to work together to spread the good news. What are you doing to build up His house?

-73-

Oneness

Object:
A dollar bill

Scripture:
I have given them the glory that you gave me, that they may be one as we are one: I in them and you in me. May they be brought to complete unity to let the world know that you sent me and have loved them even as you have loved me. Father, I want those you have given me to be with me where I am, and to see my glory, . . . Righteous Father, though the world does not know you, I know you, and they know that you have sent me. I have made you known to them, and will continue to make you known in order that the love you have for me may be in them and that I myself may be in them.
—*John 17:22–26*

A little boy went into a candy store with his father. His dad had given him a dollar, telling him he could spend his dollar on anything he wanted: jellybeans, mints, gum, or licorice. Then storekeeper told him he could get a whole handful of anything for two dollars. The boy thought for a moment and then asked his father, "Daddy, would you get a handful of jellybeans for me?"

Sometimes our relationship with God is like that: we need Him to give us a hand. When we try to do things on our own, we end up with a pretty small portion. But with God's help, we live in abundance. "I have come that they may have life, and have it to the full," God said. Sounds like He is eager to help!

Now, do you think *abundance* means things like fancy cars, big houses, designer clothes, and bulging pocketbooks? Of course not. God is very generous, but He is not like a game show host waiting to dole out prizes. God wants us to live abundantly, overflowing with love, patience, kindness, and gentleness. Jesus said, "By this all men will know that you are my disciples, if you love one another." God is eager to help us be filled with the fruits of the Spirit, because then others recognize us as His children.

I heard a story about a little boy who was asked by his friend to come to Sunday school with him. The boy said, "I can't; I belong to another abomination."

Have you ever considered that, as God's children, we are all one? Oneness is not a denomination, but rather it means oneness of the Holy Spirit. Jesus prayed in John 17:21 "that all of them may be one, Father, just as you are in me and I am in you." What would Jesus think of all the different denominations today fighting about who has it right? I preached once that, "If you're not concerned for the lost sheep, then the Shepherd is not in you." We cannot expect the world to believe that the Father sent the Son unless the world sees the oneness of Christians!

The mark of the Christian is love—honest and observable. We should be lending one another a hand, the way God steps in to lend a hand. Paul wrote to the Galatians, "Let us do good unto all men." That means Lutherans, Episcopalians, Catholics, Methodists, Presbyterians—all abominations.

Turning Your Life Over to God

-74-

Follow Me

Object:
A whistle

Scripture:

Then came the Feast of Dedication. . . . Jesus was in the temple . . . and the Jews gathered around him, saying, "How long will you keep us in suspense? If you are the Christ, tell us plainly." Jesus answered, "I did tell you, but you do not believe. The miracles I do in my Father's name speak for me, but you do not believe because you are not my sheep. My sheep listen to my voice; . . . they follow me. I give them eternal life, and they shall never perish; no one can snatch them out of my hand. . . . I and the Father are one." Again the Jews picked up stones to stone him, but Jesus said to them, "I have shown you many great miracles from the Father. For which of these do you stone me?" "We are not stoning you for any of these," replied the Jews, "but for blasphemy, because you, a mere man, claim to be God." Jesus answered them, ". . . Why then do you accuse me of blasphemy because I said, 'I am God's Son'? Do not believe me unless I do what my Father does. But if I do it, even though you do not believe me, believe the miracles, that you may know and understand that the Father is in me, and I in the Father." Again they tried to seize him, but He escaped their grasp. Then Jesus went back across the Jordan to the place where John had been baptizing in the early days. Here he stayed, and many people came to him. They said, "Though John never performed a miraculous sign, all that John said about this man was true." And in that place many believed in Jesus.

—John 10:22–42

What is your reaction to hearing a whistle? Your ears perk up. Maybe you turn your head in the direction of the sound. Do you feel a little alarmed?

A whistle is used most frequently as a warning or call to attention. Lifeguards, coaches, young women, parents, and counselors all use one. I used a whistle many years ago when I taught swimming. I used it to call the boys and girls into the life rafts, or onto the shore or pier. It made them accountable, because we had a buddy system where each person had to keep track of a buddy. If your buddy went under, you called for help.

God calls us too, through many different methods. The first and less jarring call is baptism. Many of us are baptized as children, through the church, in a sweet little ceremony. From this point on He continues to call us through His Word, and this time around, He holds us accountable. The church is our own buddy system. If one person strays away, many others can follow behind to bring him back.

At the Feast of the Dedication, the Jews were celebrating the purification of the temple, which had been desecrated by Antiochus Epiphanes. Jesus had recently performed a number of miracles, such as giving sight to a blind man. Still, the Jews doubted him. Jesus couldn't have blown a whistle any louder— his miracles in and of themselves indicated godliness. It took the good word—the accountability—of John the Baptist for people to start believing.

It's easy to call yourself a Christian. It's easy to heed God's call every week when you take Communion. But when God calls on you for something great, will you follow?

-75-

Your Sons and Daughters

Object:
Cutting the cords of the emperor moth

Scripture:

The word of the Lord came to me, saying, "Before I formed you in the womb I knew you, before you were born I set you apart; I appointed you as a prophet to the nations." "Ah, Sovereign Lord," I said, "I do not know how to speak; I am only a child." But the Lord said to me, "Do not say, 'I am only a child.' You must go to everyone I send you to and say whatever I command you. Do not be afraid of them, for I am with you and will rescue you," declares the Lord. Then the Lord reached out his hand and touched my mouth and said to me, "Now, I have put my words in your mouth. See, today I appoint you over nations and kingdoms to uproot and tear down, to destroy and overthrow, to build and to plant."

—Jeremiah 1:4–10

Mrs. Cowman had been watching a giant emperor moth come out of its cocoon for what seemed like ages. She watched it for a long time, slowly coming out, one tiny strand breaking at a time. She continued to watch as it struggled to break free of the last few strands. Finally, she became impatient. With a small pair of scissors, she cut the last few strands. The giant wings unfolded, and she waited anxiously for the beautiful creature to fly away.

But it never did. It only crawled for the rest of its life. It had not completed its growth phase: the struggle to break free from the cocoon.

Young boys and girls are just like this moth. As they grow up, they often struggle to break ties with Mom and Dad. They face the trials and tribulations of adolescence in the safety of their childhood homes, and once they've reached maturity, they are ready to leave. Like a chick slowly pecking holes in its shell, children takes small steps to maturity. They may make mistakes, turning to their parents for guidance, but eventually, they must learn to make decisions for themselves.

When Jeremiah received the call from the Lord, he reacted quickly. At first, his own immaturity humbled him. But the overwhelming presence of God touched his life, and he stepped up to the challenge. In the end, he prophesied for forty years. A prophet is not just a person who tells the future; it is also a person who speaks for God. Jeremiah knew this would be difficult, but he stepped out of his childish insularity long enough to take the call. He became a man.

Paul recalled his youth to the Corinthians: "When I was a child, I spoke like a child, I thought like a child, I reasoned like a child. When I became a man, I gave up childish ways." For both Paul and Jeremiah, there was no turning back.

Do you remember that moment when you truly felt like an adult for the first time? For many people, it's getting a driver's license or going off to college. Perhaps it was clocking in at your first job. If you're young, are you having a hard time letting go? Whatever stage you're in—whether you're nurturing still in your cocoon or you've already flown off—don't rush it. There is a time and place for everything.

-76-

The Conflict and the Victory

Object:
A gun and a cross

Scripture:

One day as he was teaching the people in the temple courts and preaching the gospel, the chief priests and the teachers of the law, together with the elders, came up to him. "Tell us by what authority you are doing these things," they said. "Who gave you this authority?" He replied, "I will also ask you a question. Tell me, John's baptism—was it from heaven, or from men?" They discussed it among themselves and said, "If we say, 'From heaven,' he will ask, 'Why didn't you believe him?' But if we say, 'From men,' all the people will stone us, because they are persuaded that John was a prophet." So they answered, "We don't know where it was from." Jesus said, "Neither will I tell you by what authority I am doing these things."

—Luke 20:1–4

Most people have a very strong reaction to seeing a gun. Someone who is a hunter might actually get excited with anticipation; others will likely recoil in fear. Either way, this reaction stems from the fact that a gun can take a life in a

189

matter of seconds. It maintains temporary control by fear; he who holds the gun, holds the power.

A cross can also take your life, but in a different way. If you devote your life to love, service, and sacrifice, you will be filled up; you won't have time for other, worldly pursuits. What is God's solution for the world? How does He suggest we can create a world of peace and brotherhood? "Take up your cross and follow me."

The ultimate conflict is to choose between the wisdom and power of man, or the wisdom and power of God. The choice is personal.

Conflict seems to be the very nature of man; each of us faces conflict every day. It is nothing new. Paul said, "For what I want to do I do not do, but what I hate I do. And if I do what I do not want to do, I agree that the law is good."

This chapter in Luke begins the final week of Jesus's life. The conflict stems from the questioning of authority: The chief priests and the teachers of the law, together with the elders, came up to him. "Tell us by what authority you are doing these things," they said. "Who gave you this authority?" Jesus responds by bringing up the authority of John the Baptist, forcing the men to admit that they didn't know where he got his authority. To help them understand, he told a parable: A man planted a vineyard and let it out to tenants while he left for some time to go to another country. While he was gone, the tenants killed a servant who came to receive some of the fruits. When the owner's son arrived, the tenants killed him as well, hoping that in killing the heir to the estate, they would receive the inheritance. The result? When the owner returned, he killed the tenants and gave the land to others.

This parable demonstrates the source of conflict: men versus God. In their shortsightedness, the men saw only themselves.

We are not completely changed today—we can't always see that far ahead. Still, there are things we can do to alleviate conflict. If we look to God for guidance, we are more likely to make decisions that will reflect the Holy Spirit inside of us.

-77-

The Touch of God

Object:
A football

Scripture:

In the beginning was the Word, and the Word was with God, and the Word was God. He was with God in the beginning. . . . The Word became flesh and made his dwelling among us. We have seen His glory, the glory of the One and Only, who came from the Father, full of grace and truth.

—*John 1:1–2, 14*

Football is one of the most popular sports in the country. Every year, the Super Bowl receives the highest ratings of any televised event. Quarterbacks are worshipped on college campuses. Thousands of teams—professional and college-level—provoke fans to astonishing levels of enthusiasm: some fans make signs, paint their bodies in team colors, drink heavily, and even get into bar brawls, all for the sake of defending their favorite team.

There are lessons to be learned from football. The first lesson has to do with teamwork. All of the players on the team do not have the same skills or do the same job. Some run, some kick, some block, some pass, and some receive. Our Savior has always relied on teamwork; he appointed a team of twelve apostles to work together under His training. Today, every country of the world is hearing about the Savior because of the teamwork of Christians; we are preaching, singing, building, teaching—all of us using our talents to spread the message of God.

Football also teaches us about interference. An offensive player with the ball is trying to reach the goal, but defensive players try everything to keep him from making it there. Other players on the offense block, run interference, and do everything they can to protect the ball carrier from tacklers. Our Savior has us running toward a goal, but Satan and his team are trying to stop us from getting there. There is not just one person carrying the ball—we all help one another to reach the goal and run interference against the devil's tacklers.

Finally, football teaches us about rules. If the game had no rules, the players would all be running helplessly on the field. So it is with us, we must live our life according to God's rules. One of the most important of these is the commandment and golden rule, "Do unto others as you would have them do unto you."

The Bible is God's Word; its purpose is to tell us about the Savior, the Christ. The result is to establish the goal—Heaven—for those who believe. Like football, there is a big difference between playing and watching. There are many Christians who play the game: they go to church, they pray, they worship, they read their Bibles, they serve their community, they attend missions. There are also Christians who sit and watch: the armchair quarterbacks and spectators. They watch while everyone else grows spiritually and does all the work.

But God calls us to be on His team. He didn't send His only Son to die so that we would sit and watch from the sidelines. Are you in the game?

-78-

Released from Captivity

Object:
A cloth caterpillar that folds into a butterfly

Scripture:

Therefore, if anyone is in Christ, he is a new creation; the old has gone, the new has come.

—*2 Corinthians 5:17*

I always felt a little sad when I saw people in the park with butterfly nets. You know those butterflies used to be caterpillars, right? You've seen them around. They inch along slowly, likely making more than a few people squirm. The view from the ground is probably quite limited; it probably sees little more than the next leaf. Finally, though, it builds a cocoon—a chrysalis. It sheds the layers of its old life, and it is no longer a worm. After this metamorphosis, a new creature emerges: a beautiful butterfly. Charlie the caterpillar is no longer confined to the sidewalk. As a butterfly, he can fly thousands of miles and has a whole new perspective of the world.

Before we come to know Christ, we are a lot like the caterpillar: we are earthbound, and we live a very limited life.

With the Holy Spirit in us, however, we are born again with the germ of eternal life. Jesus gave us His word: "He who believes in me will not die." Like a butterfly exploring an entirely new world, we cannot possibly expect what God has in store for us. Paul wrote to the Corinthians, "No eye has seen, no ear has heard, no mind has conceived what God has prepared for those who love Him." With God in our lives, there is a whole new world open to us!

As humans, we are all captives of death, but Christ died to release us from that burden. Matthew wrote, "The tombs broke open and the bodies of many holy people who had died were raised to life. They came out of the tombs, and after Jesus's resurrection they went into the holy city and appeared to many people." Christ gave us victory over death, allowing us to be new creations. To do this, we have to die to our old selves (did you really want to be a caterpillar?), experience a metamorphosis in which we abandon our worldly ways, and bring God into our lives.

Many years ago, a young man asked a woman from our congregation to marry him. He was a handsome man—a gentle-man—and she was a charming young lady. When I was coun-seling them prior to the wedding, I shared my views about who Christ is, and about His purpose on Earth. The man touched my arm and said, "I don't know what you're talking about." He had been brought up without a church connection; it seemed this was a sensitive subject for him. Shortly after that conversa-tion, he committed his life to Christ, and I performed the wed-ding service. He died a few years later at the age of twenty-eight.

Death is more than physical, however. Before our conver-sation that day, he was spiritually dead. He was like the caterpillar, inching slowly through life. When he brought Jesus into his life, he was born again; he was alive for the first time. Though he died a few years later, we know he lives on.

Have you gone through a metamorphosis? If you're still a caterpillar, make the change today. It's never too late to start living.

-79-

The Turning Point

Object:
A kernel of corn

Scripture:

You did not choose me, but I chose you and appointed you to go and bear fruit—fruit that will last. Then the Father will give you whatever you ask in my name.

—*John 15:16*

Think about a kernel of corn. It doesn't look like much—just a small, little thing. Under the right conditions, however—if it is planted in good soil, receives rain, and is kept away from weeds—that tiny kernel can yield a huge ear of corn. That ear of corn will in turn yield hundreds of new kernels.

Somewhere along the line, there was a turning point: a kernel that was worth nothing became a delicious corn crop. Jesus said the Word of God is like that seed: if it is planted in good soil, it will yield a hundredfold: "Still other seed fell on good soil, where it produced a crop—a hundred, sixty, or thirty times what was sown."

A young lady once told me a story about her roommate—we'll call her Betty. Betty and her first husband had no religious background. It wasn't necessarily that they weren't interested, they just claimed again and again that they were too busy. With all that running around, they eventually ran into problems in their marriage. They didn't know what to do, and without a faith background, divorce was an easy out. This roommate now has a new boyfriend—an ex-convict. After all these years, the couple is interested in learning about religion, but they are scared. Why? The power of evil has them entrenched. But the power of God from above is also pulling them; if they will just allow it to work on them, they will free. This could finally be the turning point.

We all have a turning point. Like the corn kernel first planted in the ground, we start off in darkness and despair, all by ourselves. We have no way of knowing about the Light from above, but slowly God eats away at our shell of pride and selfishness. As our soul is exposed, it grows upward and reaches toward the Light of life, Jesus Christ. Eventually, like the full-grown corn stalk, it is able to bear fruit of its own, continue the cycle of life by giving of itself.

Do you remember your turning point? Many of us became Christians when we were young, so we might not remember the moment when we accepted Jesus into our hearts. For others, like the woman in the story, that moment might always be very memorable. Jesus said, "Go and make disciples of all nations." So go, bear fruit, and encourage others to have their turning point.

-80-

The Most Important Guide

Object:
A map

Scripture:

Then the Lord your God will make you most prosperous in all the work of your hands and in the fruit of your womb, the young of your livestock and the crops of your land. The Lord will again delight in you and make you prosperous, just as He delighted in your fathers, if you obey the Lord your God and keep His commands and decrees that are written in this Book of the Law and turn to the Lord your God with all your heart and with all your soul.

—Deuteronomy 30:9–10

You know how Columbus thought he was sailing to India, but he went the complete opposite direction and ended up in America? That turned out great for us. I sometimes wonder what would've happened if he'd had a good map.

A map, essentially, tells us how to get from one place to another. Maybe when you were a kid you drew treasure maps—rudimentary little sketches with white chalk on black paper and a big *X* marks the spot. It was primitive, but it got you from A to B. Fast-forward to today, when cars come with GPS and iPhones can instantly redirect you when you're lost.

Of course, even the most sophisticated map is worthless if you can't read it.

God, in His grace, has provided a map for us. What is this map? The Bible, which states very clearly, "I am the way!" Easy enough to interpret, right?

Around 1250 B.C. on the edge of the Promised Land, Moses was ready to die; in fact, he had already appointed Joshua his successor. But God had a different plan for him. God came to Moses, speaking to His people through him. In this passage from Deuteronomy, Moses was explaining to his people that God would make them prosperous if they obeyed Him. Then he gave them the choice. "See, I set before you today life and prosperity, death and destruction." A or B. "For I command you today to love the Lord your God, to walk in His ways, and to keep His commands, decrees and laws; then you will live and increase, and the Lord your God will bless you in the land you are entering to possess." If they did not choose God, Moses told them, they would be destroyed.

It seems as though the people had an easy choice. But back then, they had no Bible to read, no map to follow. We've got it easy. God tells us how to love Him. Once we've made that choice, all we have to do is follow instructions.

-81-

Straight for the Sky

Object:
Trees tied down with ropes

Scripture:

Do not conform any longer to the pattern of this world, but be transformed by the renewing of your mind. Then you will be able to test and approve what God's will is—his good, pleasing, and perfect will.

—Romans 12:2

Have you ever been to Jasper National Park in Canada? Nestled in that beautiful park, there is a grove of trees growing into all sorts of twisted shapes. Some trappers went through this area many years ago, and for a want of something to do, they used a rope to tie down some small trees that were just beginning to grow. Obviously, a tree naturally wants to grow up straight and tall. But because these were tied down, they grew straight at angles from where they were tied down. The result? An entire grove of big trees growing into strange shapes.

Like the trappers that obstructed the growth of these trees, many things will come into our lives today and shape us. People with bitterness in their hearts leech onto us, eager for us to adopt their angry lifestyle. Drug dealers may tempt you with their poison. And the world is full of people who reject God; they are eager to turn us against Him.

But God wants us to grow in His direction: tall and straight.

Several years ago I read an article from *Science of Mind* magazine; it helped explain the battle that is going on all around the world for the souls of millions. There is a basic conflict: the Hebrew Bible depicts God in very human terms, but the New Testament writers declared that God is "spirit and love." John wrote, "Whoever does not love does not know God; for God is love." Semitic biblical scholars gave God human characteristics so that their people would understand the spiritual energies at work in nature and humankind. Unfortunately, after years of seeing God as angry, hateful, sorry, repentant, jealous, judging, and punitive, many religious leaders and people in the eastern and western worlds now believe that God is like this.

Since we know what God is really like, we can live our lives in accordance to His will. We don't need to conform to any tempters or faithless people who try to tie us down. We have every resource at our disposal—the Bible, family, friends, the church, service, and prayer—to allow us to grow straight up toward God.

-82-

The Shepherd Leads the Way

Object:
A shepherd's staff

Scripture:

I am the good shepherd; I know my sheep and my sheep know me—just as the Father knows me and I know the Father—and I lay down my life for the sheep. I have other sheep that are not of this sheep pen. I must bring them also. They too will listen to my voice, and there shall be one flock and one shepherd.

—*John 10:14–16*

A woman had a heart attack and was rushed to the hospital. The next day, the doctors told her she would have a swift recovery. The woman prayed, and the Lord told her she had another thirty years to live. So she figured, Well, while I've got all this extra time, I might as well get that plastic surgery I've been wanting! So she got the works: lipo suction, a facelift, and a nose job. A few days later, walking back to the hospital for a follow-up appointment, she was hit by a truck and died instantly.

She asked the Lord, "I thought you said I had another thirty years to live!"

God answered her, "I did not recognize you."

Since we have moved away from an agricultural society, many of you may not be familiar with a shepherd's staff. It is long and sturdy, with a crook on the top, meant to fend off wild animals that attempt to kill the sheep. It is also used for counting, protecting, and guiding. Sometimes, for example, the shepherd has a lamb that will not follow the flock. It wanders off because it hasn't learned to stay with the group. So the shepherd will break its leg and carry the lamb on his shoulders until it is healed. From that day forward, the lamb will never leave its shepherd.

We too have a Shepherd. Sometimes we go astray, and God has to jerk us back with His staff. Sometimes, our spirit is broken, and God has to carry us until we learn to rely on Him. Eventually, we learn that He will not leave us and that He will guard us from danger, so we will follow Him.

David sang this psalm about God. "The Lord is my shepherd, I shall not be in want. . . . He leads me beside quiet waters, He restores my soul. He guides me in paths of righteousness for His name's sake." He restores us, guides us, breaks us, and carries us because He wants us for His own.

Jesus said, "I have other sheep not of this pen." The wonderful message of the Bible is that God has opened up the door of eternal salvation for all nations and peoples and languages. All we have to do is follow Him.

-83-

Prayer Connections

Object:
Small black dots on a piece of paper

Scripture:
And pray in the Spirit on all occasions with all kinds of prayers and requests. With this in mind, be alert and always keep on praying for all the saints.

—Ephesians 6:18

Imagine a piece of paper with little black dots scattered all over it. Now take a pencil and draw stems on a few of them. On some of the dots, draw stems and connect them. Step back and look at what you've got: a musical masterpiece! (Well, maybe it's not quite Mozart, but you've a few quarter notes and eighth notes.) The idea is, with the help of a composer to draw a few simple lines, you can go from nothing to something.

God is like the composer in our lives. He takes all the little black spots and changes them into a masterpiece.

I heard a really great story about an elderly man who was an all-around fixer—he could repair anything! In his workshop he had the tools to work miracles, so people would call from miles and miles away to get help with their problems. He loved what he did so much, his wife could even hear him whistling as he worked. He truly cherished his simple life. Then one day he had a stroke. He became sullen and silent. Eventually, the calls stopped, and his wife, distraught, told everyone that he could not help them anymore. One morning a stray cat took up shelter in his workshop and gave birth to a kitten. The mother disappeared, so the man's wife took it upon herself to care for the kitten, improvising a bottle and a small bed. The kitten really took to the old man: as it grew, it would follow him everywhere, and whenever he sat down it would lie cradled in his arms, perfectly content. The little cat and the old man eventually became inseparable. One day, the wife heard her husband whistling again.

Can you understand why such a small amount of kindness to a stray cat had the healing effect that it did?

God uses different means to heal us, comfort us, and teach us. Sometimes, He chooses to make the less obvious connection. You might not think that a kitten could heal a man who had a stroke. As it turns out, having that kitten around forced that man to love again, after all that time of sulking and hiding away.

One way Jesus connected us to the Almighty God was to teach us to pray. Not only did He teach us to pray often, but also He taught us *how* to pray. "Our Father, who art in Heaven, hallowed be thy name" he taught, reminding us to revere the name of God. In praying this prayer, among others, we remain connected to God, and He can work through us.

God is a very talented composer. Are you letting Him connect the dots in your life?

-84-

It is Written!

Object:
A cell phone

Scripture:

This is the confidence we have in approaching God: that if we ask anything according to His will, He hears us. And if we know that He hears us—whatever we ask—we know that we have what we asked of Him.

—*1 John 5:14–15*

Think about how you learned to communicate: When you were a baby, you let your mother know your wants and needs by crying. Once you learned to speak, you could communicate your feelings more explicitly. Then you learned the ABCs, probably not realizing back then how important they were. Soon after, you learned to combine those letters into words; you could read and write.

Now think about all the different ways you communicate with people. You can write a letter. Not a lot of people do that anymore—it takes a little more effort, and the delivery time is a bit longer. Sending an e-mail is a little bit quicker. It sends instantly, but you still have to wait for the other person to respond. So maybe you send a text message. Even then, like the first two examples, you may never get a response. Your message is complete once you put it in the mailbox or press send. If you want immediate results, however, you can make a phone call. When you dial someone's phone number, the call is not complete until the other person picks up; you need two parties to communicate.

The way we communicate with God is through prayer. God said, "Ask and you will receive."

The way God communicates with us is through His Word. The Bible has been telling people how to live for thousands of years; the English alphabet is only a recent addition. In fact, written language in general is only about three thousand years old. Hebrew was a picture language, evolved from Egyptian hieroglyphs back when the Hebrews were slaves. Before written language, the Hebrews simply memorized the thoughts and deeds of the men and women who had been communicating with God for almost a thousand years. They lived primitively; they did not need fancy means.

The Bible, when it was finally written down, was inspired by the men and women who had been communicating with God. It tells the stories of the people who lived thousands of years ago, but it speaks to man today: right here, right now.

God's Word tells us how to live our lives. We can read it as often as we like. But sometimes God has more news. Have you ever gotten a phone call from God? He occasionally interrupts our lives when He has an urgent message for us. He doesn't want to bother with snail mail—His needs are too important to worry about us not responding. When He calls, do you answer?

-85-

Spiritual Muscles

Object:
A barbell

Scripture:

Jesus left there and went to his hometown, accompanied by his disciples. When the Sabbath came, He began to teach in the synagogue, and many who heard Him were amazed. "Where did this man get these things?" they asked. "What's this wisdom that has been given Him, that He even does miracles! Isn't this the carpenter? Isn't this Mary's son and the brother of James, Joseph, Judas, and Simon? Aren't His sisters here with us?" And they took offense at Him. Jesus said to them, "Only in His hometown, among His relatives and in His own house is a prophet without honor." He could not do any miracles there, except lay his hands on a few sick people and heal them. And He was amazed at their lack of faith.
—Mark 6:1–6

Have you ever watched the Mr. America contests? Those men are strong! I can't imagine lifting those heavy weights that they do.

Let's think about why people lift weights. They do it to strengthen their muscles. They start small and gradually move up in small increments until they can lift the desired amount. As their muscles grow bigger, they are able to carry heavier loads.

As Christians, we start off small as well. We are baptized and dedicated to God, but at that point we know very little, and we probably couldn't handle any of the temptations or heavy burdens that life throws at us. At that point, we are like a bodybuilder just beginning his training. But we learn a little bit every day; in small increments we begin to eat, and crawl, and walk, and talk. As we learn about God, we learn more about ourselves; we become more confident the stronger we get. We find out that God loves us and that He died for us.

When we are little babies, our needs are purely selfish. We want what we want, when we want it. But as our spiritual muscles grow, our love for God and others grows. We can carry more weight, and that includes the ability to empathize and care for others.

Have you ever wondered exactly who you are? Why you are here in this world? Do you have a greater purpose than just working a steady job, finding a great spouse, and raising good children? I remember one day when I was a little boy, I was coming home from church and it just struck me suddenly: Jesus lived! He was not just some person in a book, but He was a man who lived and died for us. I knew then there was more to my life.

That extra dimension we crave is the God dimension. 1 Corinthians 2:7 says, "No, we speak of God's secret wisdom, a wisdom that has been hidden and that God destined for our glory before time began." There is a yearning within us to be exalted and to be like God. The result can be completely man-centered or completely Christ-centered.

So how will you be exalted? Will you be raised up on human terms? Or will you exercise your spiritual muscles and be exalted as an obedient child of God?

-86-

Back to Life

Object:

A branch of a tree

Scripture:

On the evening of that first day of the week, when the disciples were together, with the doors locked for fear of the Jews, Jesus came and stood among them and said, "Peace be with you!" After he said this, he showed them His hands and side. The disciples were overjoyed when they saw the Lord. Again Jesus said, "Peace be with you! As the Father has sent me, I am sending you."

—*John 20:19–21*

Remember what the trees look like in midwinter? The leaves are gone, and the branches are covered in snow. The scene is very quiet. There are no signs of life.

When the weather warms up, however, that tree comes alive again. The branch buds, and with that come leaves and flowers.

We are like that branch: We have life within us, even though often we don't show it. We need the warmth and the love and the forgiveness of Jesus to help us come alive again.

That's what Jesus meant when he said, "You must be born again." We grow and bear fruit for the kingdom, meaning that we love other people so much they want to know all about Jesus themselves.

Today we are in an entirely new era of information and dramatic change. Drugs are a curse and a blessing. We can save millions of lives with medical technology. Information travels at rapid speed. And recently, we have seen some unbelievable engineering marvels. Amidst all this abundance, however, we have shortages. People are starving all over the world, and still millions more suffer violence at the hands of their leaders and fellow citizens. We are also suffering spiritual shortages.

What do we do in light of this? Let's turn to history. Change was the scene in Jesus's day, just as it is today. The three short years of His ministry came to fulfillment on Good Friday and Easter: the new faith took hold in that locked upper room when Jesus came and stood among the disciples. "I can lay my life down and I can take it up again," He said. This was a radical concept; no one had ever seen a mere man rise from the dead! But Jesus was not a mere man—He was God. So He told them, "Peace be with you! As the Father has sent me, I am sending you." Then He breathed on them and gave them the Holy Spirit, and with that, the Church began.

We all have down times—weeks or months or even years when we are spiritually dormant. We are not dead, we just need Jesus to breathe life into us. He is perfectly capable of bringing us back from a time of slumber; we must keep our minds and hearts open to understand God's power.

Think about which season it is in your life right now. Have you been lying dormant for some time, like the branch with snow on it? Are you ready to take action to melt it? There are leaves and flowers waiting to bloom underneath!

-87-

The Plan of God

Scripture:

For we are God's workmanship, created in Christ Jesus to do good works, which God prepared in advance for us to do.

—*Ephesians 2:10*

Do you have a beautiful rug in your home? Colorful and intricately designed? Perhaps your friends and neighbors even give you compliments. A great rug can be the centerpiece of a room, because the rest of the furniture complements and enhances it.

Now have you ever looked at the underside of that rug? It looks like a completely different piece of tapestry! There are loose threads everywhere, and there is no discernible pattern or color scheme.

As Christians, our lives are very much like that chaotic hidden side of the rug: From our vantage point, all we can see are the little moments, day after day, a routine that appears to have very little loveliness or direction. Sometimes it's hard to keep going when it seems as though everything is unraveling. But God can see the beautiful pattern on top; He has a grand plan. He is the Weaver.

A student of mine at Midland College wrote these words:

My life is but a weaving, between my Lord and me.
I cannot choose the colors, nor all the patterns, see.
Sometimes He chooses sorrow, and I, in foolish pride,
Forget He sees the upper, and I the underside
Not till the loom is silent, and the shuttles cease to fly
Will He reveal the pattern or tell the reason why.
The dark threads are needful in the Weaver's skillful hand,
As the threads of gold and silver in the pattern He has planned.

Do you ever get that feeling that if you just pull on the threads, maybe you'll be able to peek through and see the big picture? Do you ever get overwhelmed at how dark the colors are down there, or how knotty the threads are? When you begin to feel that way, it's important to remember what's on the other side: a beautiful pattern of perfectly arranged shapes and colors. God took His time weaving the rug that is your life; He didn't just toss it together haphazardly (even though it looks that way from your perspective).

Imagine you lost your job. You're angry, and you can't for the life of you see why God wanted this to happen (all you see are all the ugly knots on the bottom of the rug!). But then that opens a few doors for you—you end up finding a new job for which you're better suited, and now you're more fulfilled and can provide more for your family. That's the other side of the rug that you just couldn't see before.

"I tell you the truth," Jesus said, "anyone who has faith in me will do what I have been doing. He will do even greater things than these . . ." We've all been in that place where we feel directionless. But Jesus told us explicitly that with faith, we *will* do good works. God does have a plan for our lives, but we must surrender to Him.

It takes a great deal of faith to surrender and accept what God has planned. But just imagine how great it will feel when you finally see the big picture!

-88-

Response

Object:
Music

Scripture:
The people walking in darkness have seen a great Light.

—Isaiah 9:2

Think about all the different occasions that you hear music: In your car on the way to work. Waiting in line for your morning coffee. In the lobby at the bank. At a wedding reception. At a funeral. On your friend's patio. At a concert. On Sunday morning at church. Everywhere! We've gotten so accustomed to music playing constantly that we don't even notice it half the time. Can you imagine a world without music? How quiet that would be?

Many years ago I read an article by Louis Cassels called "Star." In it he described a college professor who had come up with a modern way to thank God. He brought his congregants into a room together, turned all the lights off, and filled the room with music from a stereophonic record. It was music— you couldn't see it, feel it, or touch it. The fact that it was dark only heightened that sensation. It filled the whole room, permeated their beings. None of them had ever experienced anything like this; they were changed by this new form of expression.

Have any of you ever been this moved by music? I'm sure you have. I know how people dance at clubs and bang their heads at concerts. I've seen people sing in their cars. Perhaps you remember very vividly your favorite concert. Did the Eagles or the Stones ever move you to tears? Make you want to raise your hands and scream praise?

Let's talk about response. God calls on us, and we need to respond. Consider the Bible. The Old Testament is full of prophecy, and the New Testament is the fulfillment. Would it have meant anything if those prophecies went unfulfilled? The Old Testament can be very intimidating with all its talk of judgment. Luckily for us, God pulled through: "The Word became flesh and made his dwelling among us." The New Testament is comforting, as it tells us about salvation. The catch? Man, with free will, can make the choice to respond to God's gift.

Isaiah 9:2 says, "The people walking in darkness have seen a great Light. On those living in the land of the shadow of death, a Light has shined." This tells us that man's natural condition is one of judgment. Matthew quotes this later in the New Testament, and Mark tells us, "He who does not believe is condemned." So what do we do to avoid judgment and condemnation? We respond to God's great sacrifice; we turn our lives over to Christ.

Think about the music you listen to: the music you hear on the radio on the way to church versus the hymns you sing when you get there. Maybe you're singing along in the car, really getting into that Bob Dylan song. But then when you get to church, do you just sing along automatically? Do you sing

"Were You There When They Crucified My Lord" without recognizing the significance? At some point, if you listen hard enough, God's message will bring you to your knees. Think about how you've been responding to God. Are you allowing Him to really move you?

-89-

Called, Consecrated, and Sent!

Object:
A beeper

Scripture:

And the God of all grace, who called you to His eternal glory in Christ, after you have suffered a little while, will Himself restore you and make you strong, firm, and steadfast.

—1 Peter 5:10

What do you do when you want to send someone a message? If that person lives nearby, you can drop in and deliver the message in person. You can call on the phone. Or you can send an e-mail or text message.

But what about beepers? Remember those? You wore the little device on your hip, and if someone needed to reach you, he would send you a page with his phone number on it. Then you'd find the nearest public phone booth and call him. Seems pretty straightforward, right? Until cell phones became popular in the nineties, this was all we had!

God calls us too. He beeps into our lives every now and then with a gentle reminder if He wants to send us somewhere or if He wants us to do something special. But how does He do this? God doesn't have a phone number!

God is pretty inventive; He has several methods of getting in touch. God calls us through the Bible, or through a sermon or prayer. He also calls us through the Holy Spirit. When we connect with the Lord God, we connect with the greatest power in the world. That power is love. He continually beeps us through these methods to keep us on our feet, because He wants us to have a wonderful life of joy and abundance.

When God wants us to do something, He has to get our attention first; that's the call. As 1 Peter says, God called us "to His eternal glory in Christ." God calls us so that we will glorify His Son, and that we in turn will be glorified by the gift of eternal life. Next, we are consecrated. Christians, who have received God and believe that Jesus is the Christ, are one in the Spirit. Jesus is continually connecting us with God. He said, "For them I sanctify myself, that they too may be truly sanctified." One way we maintain this connection is through prayer, which is as vital to us as breathing. (A little boy once asked his friend why his grandma read her Bible all the time. The boy said, "She's preparing for her finals.") Finally, after we are called and consecrated, we are sent. Acts 1:8 says, "But you will receive power when the Holy Spirit comes on you; and you will be my witnesses in Jerusalem, and in all Judea and Samaria, and to the ends of the earth." This is pretty powerful. It means that God is giving us the power to change lives! There are thousands and thousands of people on this planet that will never know about God . . . until you tell them.

We're all in different places in our spiritual lives. At some point, God has surely beeped in on all of us. Maybe He called you, and you were led to take over leadership of the church choir. Maybe He called you to step up your Bible reading. Whatever it is, the important thing is that you listen. God trusts us enough to send us out into the world as messengers. When He pages, will you take action?

God's Gift

-90-

God's Generosity

Object:
An engagement ring

Scripture:

For the kingdom of heaven is like a landowner who went out early in the morning to hire men to work in his vineyard. He agreed to pay them a denarius for the day and sent them into his vineyard. About the third hour he went out and saw others standing in the marketplace doing nothing. He told them, "You will go and work in my vineyard, and I will pay you whatever is right." So they went. He went out again about the sixth hour and the ninth hour and did the same thing. About the eleventh hour he went and found still others standing around. He asked them, "Why have you been standing here all day long doing nothing?" "Because no one has hired us," they answered. He said to them, "You also go and work in my vineyard." When evening came, the owner of the vineyard said to his foreman, "Call the workers and pay them their wages, beginning with the last hired and going on to the first." The workers who were hired about the eleventh hour came and each received a denarius. So when those came who were hired first, they expected to receive more. But each one of them also received a denarius. When they received it, they began to grumble against the landowner. 'These men who were hired last worked only one hour," they said, "and you have made them equal to us who have borne the burden of the work and the heat of the day." But he answered one of them, "Friend, I am not being unfair to you. Didn't you agree to work for a denarius? Take your pay and go. I want to give the man who was hired last the same as I gave you. Don't I have the right to do what I want with my own money? Or are you envious because I am generous? So the last will be first, and the first will be last."

—Matthew 20:1–16

Did you ever get a gift you weren't expecting?—some people would call this a surprise. Was it difficult to accept, no strings attached? We reason that no gift is really free. Perhaps this surprise—given of kindness and generosity—hits your pride, and you feel compelled to give something in return. If your friend takes you out to dinner, do you say, "The next one's on me"?

Did you ever get an engagement ring? That wasn't truly free, because you were expected to provide a ring for your husband in return.

God gave us a gift that truly has no strings attached. What's the catch? We have to ask for it. This gift is greater than any diamond or fancy dress or expensive vacation—He gave us the gift of His only son, Jesus. When we receive him, we become children of God.

Through God's gift of His son, we receive eternal life. As in the parable, God calls us all to be His workers. He doesn't care whether we come into the fields early in the day or late at night, the reward will be the same: we all enter the kingdom of heaven. When you meet someone who has just become a Christian, do you begrudge that person? No! You are thrilled to have a new worker, a new brother in Christ, a new friend to share the reward of life eternal.

The next time someone gives you a gift, consider accepting it with a truly gracious spirit. God gave generously; it's only polite to accept.

-91-

The New Shape

Object:
An Edwardian-era lady's shoe and modern woman's shoe

Scripture:

But now a righteousness from God, apart from law, has been made known, to which the Law and the Prophets testify. This righteousness from God comes through faith in Jesus Christ to all who believe. There is no difference, for all have sinned and fall short of the glory of God, and are justified freely by his grace through the redemption that came by Christ Jesus. God presented him as a sacrifice of atonement, through faith in his blood. He did this to demonstrate his justice, because in his forbearance he had left the sins committed beforehand unpunished—he did it to demonstrate his justice at the present time, so as to be just and the one who justifies those who have faith in Jesus.

—Romans 3:21–26

It's hard to keep up with what's in style. Think about some of the fashions that were popular when you were younger. If you grew up in the fifties, maybe you wore a swing skirt and white gloves. At your prime in the sixties? Perhaps you wore seersucker and a pillbox hat. In the eighties you probably wore stirrup pants, Wayfarer sunglasses, and oversized paint splatter shirts. But what about shoes—something we always need? Women in the early twentieth century wore very pointy shoes that laced all the way up their ankle. Things have changed slightly—you women still wear extremely pointy and uncomfortable shoes, but they've taken on a more dainty shape. They also come in more colors and varieties. But what still goes inside a shoe? Your foot.

The foot is the same as it always has been—inside the shoe you've got the same five toes—but the outside is just decorated differently. The Reformation of the church was very similar. The Gospel is the same; we merely gave it a new presentation. No matter what time or place, the Gospel never changes.

In the sixteenth century, the Roman Catholic Church was a secular, worldly power. It reached every nation, directly or indirectly. Leading up to the Reformation, the Church went through three very different periods: dissemination, domination, and disintegration. Missionaries supported themselves in the beginning, spreading the Word, until the Church became a theocracy, indulgences were common practice, and the Crusades terrified people everywhere. People demanded change.

In 1517, Martin Luther posted the Ninety-Five Theses, blasphemously (at the time) suggesting that salvation did not come from good works, but that it was a free gift from God. He translated the Bible from Latin into a language the people could understand, making it more accessible. The Church was reformed and reshaped, but the core message remained unchanged: God still sent His Son to die for you, so that you can have eternal life.

The Church is still being reformed and reshaped today. Scientists around the world are researching the God dimension. Laymen and clergymen from all denominations are cooperating. We must be alert to the changing needs of our Church, so that we can answer when God calls us.

-92-

Magic or Miracle?

Object:
A silk handkerchief and a fake thumb

Scripture:

Do not let your hearts be troubled. Trust in God; trust also in me. In my Father's house are many rooms; if it were not so, I would have told you. I am going there to prepare a place for you. And if I go and prepare a place for you, I will come back and take you to be with me that you also may be where I am. You know the way to the place where I am going.

—*John 14:1–4*

Has anyone ever tried to show you a magic trick? You know, guess the card, cut a woman in half, pull a rabbit out of a hat. What about the one where someone's thumb disappears and—magically—reappears? I'll let you in on the secret of that one. You wrap your fist around a fake thumb, hiding your real thumb inside your grip. Cover your hand with a handkerchief—it should look as though your thumb is sticking up in a thumbs up position. Now pull off the hanky, taking the fake thumb with it. No thumb! Magic, right?

Now that was a trick. But what about something that's pretty fantastic and perfectly legitimate? Jesus came to give us something that is real. He came into our world to help us live a life full of miracles—not tricks, but real-life changes. With Him in our life, we are new creations, with new hearts. We are like Jesus. That's not magic; that's a miracle.

Imagine you lived one hundred years ago. There was no FM radio. There was no television. No microwaves. No jet airplanes. No atomic energy. No digital cameras. No space flights. No disposable diapers. No bubble gum. No zippers. No cell phones. No Internet. No iPods.

Now try to imagine what Heaven is like. Paul wrote in his first letter to the Corinthians that "No eye has seen, no ear has heard, no mind has conceived what God has prepared for those who love Him." So even if we try to imagine it, we can't. It's that incredible. We have to go on faith, trusting what Jesus told us: "I have prepared a place for you." Here we learn two things: that we will be individuals in the next life, recognizable to our loved ones, and that Heaven is a very definite place already in existence.

It's no trick. Do you believe it?

-93-

Manifested

Object:
Hands

Scripture:

Don't you believe that I am in the Father, and that the Father is in me? The words I say to you are not just my own. Rather, it is the Father, living in me, who is doing His work. Believe me when I say that I am in the Father and the Father is in me; or at least believe on the evidence of the miracles themselves. I tell you the truth, anyone who has faith in me will do what I have been doing. He will do even greater things than these, because I am going to the Father.

—*John 14:10–12*

Some social scientists say that our hands are what distinguish us from animals (we have opposable thumbs). With our hands we can perform the most intricate movements; we can create the finest watches, paint a beautiful masterpiece, give a soothing massage, wave good-bye to a friend, help a person up from the ground, play a piano concerto, or prepare a delectable meal. But with our hands we can also shoot a gun, detonate a bomb, forge a check, or throw a punch. Behind the hands is a heart that loves or hates, a brain that sends messages to hug or hit.

As Christians we can do a lot with our hands, but only if our heart is in the right place. We are here to love thoroughly and to lift others up. We are here to make the world a better place. We can do all this only if we have Jesus in our hearts and we know Him as Lord.

The word "manifest" means to reveal. Think of it as the open hand ("mani" means hand). When the hand is open, it reveals what is in the hand when it is closed.

God revealed Himself in His son, Jesus. "Anyone who has seen me has seen the Father," Jesus said to his disciples. If God is in Jesus, we can look to Jesus to learn about God. So what do we see in Jesus? We see love, sensitivity, and warmth, as He held little children in His lap. We see compassion, which He bestowed upon sinners, beggars, the hungry, and the dying. We see power because He could forgive sins, calm the storm, raise Lazarus from the dead, and feed the masses. We see healing because He gave sight to the blind. And finally, we see salvation because we are told that whoever believes in Him will not perish. We see in Jesus what humans are not: God revealed, manifested.

Are you motivated to use your hands for good? With a pure heart and the intention to serve God, there is so much you can do. You can build a house for a family in need. You can play worship music for children who have never heard it. You can give a Bible to someone who doesn't have one. In doing these things, other people might just see God manifested in you.

-94-

Breaking Trail

Object:
A snowshoe

Scripture:

In those days John the Baptist came, preaching in the Desert of Judea and saying, "Repent, for the kingdom of heaven is near." . . . People went out to him from Jerusalem and all Judea and the whole region of the Jordan. Confessing their sins, they were baptized by him in the Jordan River. But when he saw many of the Pharisees and Sadducees coming . . . he said to them: "You brood of vipers! Who warned you to flee from the coming wrath? Produce fruit in keeping with repentance. And do not think you can say to yourselves, 'We have Abraham as our father.' I tell you that out of these stones God can raise up children for Abraham. The ax is already at the root of the trees, and every tree that does not produce good fruit will be cut down and thrown into the fire. "I baptize you with water for repentance. But after me will come one who is more powerful than I, whose sandals I am not fit to carry. He will baptize you with the Holy Spirit and with fire. His winnowing fork is in His hand, and He will clear His threshing floor, gathering His wheat into the barn and burning up the chaff with unquenchable fire."

— Matthew 3:1–12

A snowshoe is different from the other shoes we wear on our feet. Some shoes are for comfort. Some are for sport. Some are meant to add height and attract attention. A snowshoe is none of these things; it is large, flat, and light, fastened to the foot with straps so that the foot can move back and forth as the person walks. It is designed to keep the person wearing it from sinking into deep snow. In effect, it is a life-saving tool.

God has given us something to "wear" when we're in a snowstorm; He would hate for us to give up and sink. The snowshoe He has given us is faith.

We used snowshoes in Arctic Survival School back when I was in the service. When it would snow heavily, we would send someone ahead of the group with a pack and snowshoes to "break trail." It was hard work: this person would sink down and then have to lift his legs high so that he could take the next difficult step. Even in below zero weather, we were perspiring because we each carried a sixty- to eighty-pound pack. Whoever it was that broke trail really took one for the team, because his sacrifice made it easier for the rest of us to walk the trail.

John the Baptist broke the trail for Jesus. He was born in a small town in Jerusalem just six months before Jesus. At the time, Pontius Pilate was the Roman governor and Caiaphas was the high priest; King Herod ruled Galilee wickedly. yet efficiently. John grew up to be a great prophet: he lived ascetically, challenged sinful rulers, called for repentance, and promised God's justice. His preaching prepared people for the message of Jesus; in fact, John's followers eventually merged into Jesus's disciples. Significantly, it was John who recognized Jesus as Messiah and baptized him.

John took on a heavy burden by preparing the world for Jesus. We too have people in our lives who break the trail for us. Our parents provide shelter, feed us, and love us. When we are grown, we return the favor. Are you prepared to go forward?

-95-

Out of Darkness (Easter sermon)

Object:
A trick candle

Scripture:

Then the disciples went back to their homes, but Mary stood outside the tomb crying. As she wept, she bent over to look into the tomb and saw two angels in white, seated where Jesus's body had been, one at the head and the other at the foot. They asked her, "Woman, why are you crying?" "They have taken my Lord away," she said, "and I don't know where they have put him." At this, she turned around and saw Jesus standing there, but she did not realize that it was Jesus. "Woman," He said, "why are you crying? Who is it you are looking for?" Thinking he was the gardener, she said, "Sir, if you have carried him away, tell me where you have put him, and I will get him." Jesus said to her, "Mary." She turned toward Him and cried out in Aramaic, "Rabboni!" . . . Jesus said, "Do not hold on to me, for I have not yet returned to the Father. Go instead to my brothers and tell them, 'I am returning to my Father and your Father, to my God and your God.'" Mary Magdalene went to the disciples with the news: "I have seen the Lord!"

—John 20:10–18

Did you ever try to blow out candles on your birthday cake, and you couldn't? No matter how hard you blew on them, they stayed lit! Some trickster—maybe your big brother—put trick candles on your cake. These candles relight themselves, the principle being that by igniting magnesium inserted into the wick of the candle, the vapor given off when a candle is blown out can be set alight, and the candle can reignite.

Jesus is like this trick candle. The world was a dark place, but it could not dampen His light. He faced a cruel mob, He was tortured, and He was strung up on a wooden cross to die. But He conquered death. He first appeared to Mary Magdalene, a woman who had been full of evil and sin, like mankind stumbling directionless through the dark. But Christ rose from his dark tomb of death and appeared to her, redeeming her and transforming her into a symbol of hope.

Isaiah, speaking of the Messiah, said "I have called you . . . to be a covenant for the people and a light for the Gentiles . . . to release from the dungeon those who sit in darkness." Jesus also recognized this in Himself. He said, "I am the light of the world!" He also told his followers, "You are the light of the world!" In this world of darkness, hate, murder, and suffering, Christians are called to bring light—joy, peace, and love—to people of every nation.

Have you ever had that sensation of walking into your church after a long, hectic, stressful day? Maybe you were thinking about the world outside, or maybe you just watched the news. Then you walk into the sanctuary, and thousands of candles are lit. You realize that all the bad news and trauma and darkness of the outside world is trivial compared to the light coming from your church. Keep it burning.

-96-

Who is Jesus?

Object:
The cross

Scripture:

After six days Jesus took with him Peter, James, and John . . . and led them up a high mountain by themselves. There he was transfigured before them. His face shone like the sun, and his clothes became as white as the light. Just then there appeared before them Moses and Elijah, talking with Jesus. Peter said to Jesus, "Lord, it is good for us to be here. If you wish, I will put up three shelters—one for you, one for Moses, and one for Elijah." While he was still speaking, a bright cloud enveloped them, and a voice from the cloud said, "This is my Son, whom I love; with him I am well pleased. Listen to him!" When the disciples heard this, they fell facedown to the ground, terrified. But Jesus came and touched them. "Get up," he said. "Don't be afraid." When they looked up, they saw no one except Jesus. As they were coming down the mountain, Jesus instructed them, "Don't tell anyone what you have seen, until the Son of Man has been raised from the dead."

—Matthew 17:1–9

We all know Jesus died on the cross.; it's the most enduring symbol of Christianity. For that reason we have crosses in our homes and churches and around our necks. But have you ever thought about what it means?

The cross points in four directions. First, it points downward, into the earth. We are all going to die someday, as Jesus died on that cross many years ago. "I am the resurrection and the life!" Jesus said. But that same stake that points to the ground also points upward, to Heaven. Jesus said, "if I go and prepare a place for you, I will come back and take you to be with me that you also may be where I am." Heaven is our home forever. It is so beautiful that Paul told us we could not even conceive of what was in store for us there!

The two arms of the cross point in all directions. We are told to go and make disciples of all nations, that our actions will demonstrate to others that we are children of God. ("By this all men will know that you are my disciples, if you love one another.")

So while the horizontal part of the cross reminds us of our duty as Christians, the vertical stake tells us about Jesus. Another way to be reminded of who Jesus was is to read the Bible.

If you read the Bible right, you can be transformed. Have you ever read so deeply and thoroughly that the words on the page came to life? Our scripture is about the transfiguration of Jesus, one of the most important stories in the New Testament because it demonstrates His divinity. Peter, James, and John were witnesses. They were amazed to see Jesus's face as it "shone like the sun." They couldn't believe the sight before them, so God had to speak to them from Heaven, saying, "Listen to him." They fell to the ground, in awe of the Savior.

Every time you look down at that cross around your neck, think about what it really means. It's not just some nice piece of jewelry. It's there to remind you that God sent His only Son here to Earth, so that you could have a place in Heaven, and now you have a duty to spread that message to people all over the world.

-97-

The Perfection of Jesus

Object:
A dictionary

Scripture:

Love never fails. But where there are prophecies, they will cease; where there are tongues, they will be stilled; where there is knowledge, it will pass away. For we know in part and we prophesy in part, but when perfection comes, the imperfect disappears. When I was a child, I talked like a child, I thought like a child, I reasoned like a child. When I became a man, I put childish ways behind me. Now we see but a poor reflection as in a mirror; then we shall see face to face. Now I know in part; then I shall know fully, even as I am fully known.

—1 Corinthians 13:8–12

We've all used a dictionary at some point in our lives. Is it "complement" or "compliment"? Is it "illusive" or "elusive"? And does anyone actually know what "antidisestablishmentarianism" means?

Mark Twain joked with a friend once. He said, "I have a book at home that has every word of your speech: a dictionary." Clever fellow. But a dictionary, as helpful as it is, is really just an assortment of completely random words. The word "allotment" on page fifteen has no relation to "perambulate" on page two hundred.

The Bible comprises the exact same words that are in your dictionary at home. The difference? The words in the Bible have a lot more meaning. They are put together perfectly, divinely inspired by God. Other books lose prominence over time, but the Bible is the most widely read book in history. The Bible transcends other literature. *The True Confessions of Charlotte Doyle* was popular in the nineteenth century, but has it been circulated worldwide and translated into over a hundred languages? Have you heard of it?

We too can live on forever, if we let the Word become our life. Though it seems as though our lives are made up of random events, like words in the dictionary, it is nothing like that. God has a perfect plan for our lives, purposefully prepared in advanced.

With the advances in science and technology, we as humans tend to believe we are getting closer and closer to perfection every day. (Think of the vast differences in procedures like childbirth and cancer treatment compared to just a century ago!) Fields like psychiatry are also making huge advances as far as understanding how and why we act the way we do. But we are nowhere near perfect. The central theme of the Bible— of the New Testament at least—is Jesus Christ. He is the Son of God, the Savior of the world. History reveals how man, created in God's image, has tried again and again to become divine. But man fails every time. We have witnessed man's imperfection through centuries of bigotry, drug violence, war, financial corruption, and moral decay.

Yet still we strive constantly to be more like our great Teacher, Jesus Christ. We are told that love never fails. If we are humbled by our imperfections yet still aware that God has a great plan, we can push toward our ultimate goal: eternity with God.

-98-

And It Will Come!

Object:
A large watch with a chain

Scripture:

There will be signs in the sun, moon, and stars. On the earth, nations will be in anguish and perplexity at the roaring and tossing of the sea. Men will faint from terror, apprehensive of what is coming on the world, for the heavenly bodies will be shaken. At that time they will see the Son of Man coming in a cloud with power and great glory. When these things begin to take place, stand up and lift up your heads, because your redemption is drawing near." He told them this parable: "Look at the fig tree and all the trees. When they sprout leaves, you can see for yourselves and know that summer is near. Even so, when you see these things happening, you know that the kingdom of God is near. I tell you the truth, this generation will certainly not pass away until all these things have happened. Heaven and earth will pass away, but my words will never pass away.

—*Luke 21:25–33*

A man once joked, "What kind of world is this we live in—I asked a dozen people all day what time it was, and they all said something different!"

Time is an intriguing concept. Many of us having spent a lot of time contemplating the future. What will happen tomorrow? Next week? When we die? The hands of the clock move at the same speed, regardless of what we do. Still, it seems as though we are always running out of time.

We constantly find ourselves asking, "What time is it?" We teach our children to tell the time early on, because we really base our lives around it. *It's already 8:30? I should be awake! It's noon? I should probably eat (even if I'm not really hungry).* And *Is it 5:00 yet?*

Have you ever thought about the sequence of time in terms of the aging of man? Because of the actions of one man, death came to all men (through sin). In looking at a child, we see the beginning of life. We then see death in the third and fourth generation. We are all aware of aging; it hangs over our shoulders every day, encouraging us to try this treatment and that procedure to hang onto our youth for dear life. But are we are aware of eternity?

Our gospel lesson gives us a little insight. It begins with Jesus knowing He is going to die, so He preaches about last things to his disciples. Luke 21 begins with Jesus at the Temple. He prophesied about the destruction of the Temple, and then he foretold of His own coming. "Watch out that you are not deceived," He told them, "For many will come in my name, claiming, 'I am He,' and, 'The time is near.' Do not follow them." He even warned them that they would be persecuted. But then He comforted them: "But not a hair of your head will perish. By standing firm you will gain life." He promised them eternity.

Time is never static, and it never has been. In Jesus's day, the first hour was 6:00 a.m. The third hour was 9:00 a.m. The sixth hour was noon. Finally, the *eleventh hour* was just before the end of the day: 5:00 p.m. Thus, the term eleventh hour has always meant that there was not much time left. We are constantly made aware of how short our time here on Earth is. What are you doing with your time? Are you preparing for eternity?

-99-

Who is He?

Object:
An elephant and three blind men

Scripture:

What, then, shall we say in response to this? If God is for us, who can be against us? He who did not spare his own Son, but gave Him up for us all—how will He not also, along with Him, graciously give us all things? Who will bring any charge against those whom God has chosen? It is God who justifies. Who is He that condemns? Christ Jesus, who died—more than that, who was raised to life—is at the right hand of God and is also interceding for us. Who shall separate us from the love of Christ? Shall trouble or hardship or persecution or famine or nakedness or danger or sword?

—Romans 8:31–35

Three blind men approached an elephant. The first man bravely reached out to touch it. Feeling its tail, he said, "The elephant is like a rope." The second man stepped forward and touched the elephant's sturdy side. "The elephant is like a wall," he said. The last man stepped forward and patted the animal's leg. "No, no," he said. "The elephant is like a tree!"

We all see Christ differently, just like these three blind men all had a different perception of the elephant. Some of us see Christ as a thin lifeline of hope. Others see Christ as some impenetrable wall of mystery—they can't see the total picture. Others, perhaps, view Christ as a tree of life, something that grows tall and bears fruit. I was talking to a woman recently—a wealthy lady in a lovely home—and she told me she never thinks about the life to come. To her, Jesus is a wall that we just cannot understand. A lot of us are overwhelmed by stress, illness, bills, tragedy, and other things; our connection to Christ is a very thin line of hope. But the lifeline is still there, and we are hanging on no matter what.

So who exactly *is* Christ? We could talk about a lot of different things: the atonement, the cross, the incarnation, the virgin birth, the miracles, the parables, the sermons, the second coming. So who is He? He is past, present, and future.

The past is written for us in the Bible. The book of John begins, "In the beginning was the Word, and the Word was with God, and the Word was God. He was with God in the beginning. Through Him all things were made; without Him nothing was made that has been made. . . . The Word became flesh and made his dwelling among us." The New Testament tells the story of Jesus's redemption of mankind from sin and death.

Jesus died, but He rose again. He said, "I am the life." He is now God made known. He is here in the present for every Christian who opens his or her heart to Him. You can involve Jesus in everything you do: from waking up in the morning to driving to work to gardening to eating dinner (praying) until your head hits the pillow.

The future is for man to decide. Jesus taught, "Thy kingdom come, thy will be done on Earth as it is in Heaven." We are His workmanship, and we live in the promise of God's Word.

So who is Christ? He is the Lord of life, who died to set us free from death. He is the past, present, and future. The past is set in stone. In the present, He calls each of us to a life away from mediocrity and ease. Will you be with Him in the future?

-100-

The Beginning and the End

Object:
A circle

Scripture:

Many have undertaken to draw up an account of the things that have been fulfilled among us, just as they were handed down to us by those who from the first were eyewitnesses and servants of the word. Therefore, since I myself have carefully investigated everything from the beginning, it seemed good also to me to write an orderly account for you, most excellent Theophilus, so that you may know the certainty of the things you have been taught.

—Luke 1:1–4

Eternity has been described as a circle: no beginning and no end. It has a certain timelessness that man cannot understand. Man, however, has a very certain beginning and end. He is born, and he dies. But God gave mankind the power to become children of God, a gift that frees us from the certainty of death. At that point, man becomes an entity, a unit in himself, a part of the eternal with God. As Jesus said, "Though you die, yet shall you live," that new birth is of the Spirit of God, closing that gap.

Let's go back to the beginning. The gospel of Luke was written by the same man who wrote the book of Acts; the generally accepted date is 70 A.D., after Nero's persecution of the Christians. It was written in the popular Koine Greek, the international language of the Greco-Roman world.

Luke had several major interests in writing his gospel. He wished to show that Christianity was not a subversive sect. He also wished to support the claim that the church had superseded the true Israel and was entitled to the recognition and protection that the state had previously given to Judaism. Finally, Luke was eager to stress the fact that Christianity was a world religion and had no racial limitations.

The first thing Luke did was establish the fact that there were eyewitnesses. He wrote to Theophilus, a Greek Christian who may have been a Roman official. The meat of the gospel begins with John the Baptist; he preached to break the shell of indifference and prepare the way for Christ. Next came the Annunciation by God's messenger Gabriel, who told Mary she was to give birth to the Christ. From there Luke tells of the Christmas story, and the life and miracles of Jesus, all the way to His death and resurrection.

The important thing for us to remember is that Luke spoke of an "orderly account." Christianity is a fact of history—Christ lived and died in Palestine. Luke and the others saw firsthand these miracles. It is the Holy Spirit that verifies all of this today.

So the beginning of Luke establishes the authority of the eyewitnesses: the disciples of Christ. Then we learn the story of Jesus from beginning to end (though His story continues today). The creatures of Heaven—the messengers of light—reveal the harmony between Heaven and earth. We are closer to eternity than we can understand! The beginning always comes from God, and the ends of man's life are welded together in Christ, and we become eternal. That's pretty humbling.

About the Author

Born in Wisconsin in 1917, Rev. Henry B. Kleinert lived an adventurous youth during the height of the Depression. He went on to study pre-law and pre-med at the University of Wisconsin. In 1940, he married Helen Peck, with whom he had two children, Gary and Linda. Ever the philanthropist, Kleinert served on the Madison YMCA and served as an Arctic Survival Instructor in the army. He was also involved in the Spring Green, Wisconsin, Chamber of Commerce and was active in his church. Though he was always aware of that extra dimension in his life beyond the physical, it took the love and encouragement of his friends, family, and congregation to propel him into the ministry.

After receiving his calling, and upon the urging of dear friend and pastor Dr. Charles Puls, Kleinert attended Midland College Central Seminary in Fremont, Nebraska, eventually becoming ordained in 1953. He began his ministry at Luther Memorial in Madison, Wisconsin, that same year; he went on to preach for more than fifty years, reaching people along the way with his "everyday objects" sermons. He retired on July 18, 2004, and now lives in Texas where he can be near his children and grandchildren.